James Sibbald David Scott

To Jamaica and Back

James Sibbald David Scott

To Jamaica and Back

ISBN/EAN: 9783743410268

Manufactured in Europe, USA, Canada, Australia, Japa

Cover: Foto ©Andreas Hilbeck / pixelio.de

Manufactured and distributed by brebook publishing software (www.brebook.com)

James Sibbald David Scott

To Jamaica and Back

PAGE 74.

TO JAMAICA AND BACK

BY

Sir SIBBALD DAVID SCOTT, Bart.

"A land of streams."
TENNYSON'S *Lotos-Eaters*.

LONDON
CHAPMAN AND HALL, 193, PICCADILLY
1876

TO

MY WIFE,

AT WHOSE SUGGESTION THIS DIARY WAS WRITTEN,

𝔍 𝔇𝔢𝔡𝔦𝔠𝔞𝔱𝔢 𝔱𝔥𝔢𝔰𝔢 𝔓𝔞𝔤𝔢𝔰.

LONDON, 1875.

CONTENTS.

CHAPTER I.
UNDER WEIGH . . . . . . PAGE 1

CHAPTER II.
OUR PASSENGERS 5

CHAPTER III.
OUR SHIP 19

CHAPTER IV.
LAND AT LAST 32

CHAPTER V.
ALONG THE ISLANDS 42

CHAPTER VI.
ST. THOMAS'S.—JACMEL 54

CHAPTER VII.
JAMAICA 72

viii   *CONTENTS.*

CHAPTER VIII.
PAGE
NEWCASTLE 84

CHAPTER IX.
CATHERINE'S PEAK.—ROPLEY.—COFFEE-WORKS . . . 96

CHAPTER X.
JAMAICA 107

CHAPTER XI.
JAMAICA (*Continued*) 146

CHAPTER XII.
JAMAICA (*Continued*) 180

CHAPTER XIII.
SPANISH TOWN AND LINSTEAD 227

CHAPTER XIV.
PLANTS, VEGETABLES, AND ANIMALS.—KINGSTON AND PORT ROYAL.—THE "NILE" AGAIN 263

CHAPTER XV.
COALING.—CLOSE SHAVING.—HOMEWARD BOUND . . 299

CHAPTER XVI.
AT SEA.—AT HOME 310

TO JAMAICA AND BACK.

CHAPTER I.

UNDER WEIGH.

SEATED on a camp-stool in my cabin, with a sofa-pillow across my knees as a substitute for a table, I take my pen in hand to carry out your parting injunction to register the events of my voyage. The writing is occasionally interrupted by a lurch of the vessel, for we are arriving on the verge of the Bay of Biscay, and the rollers come with a bang on the quarter, as though they wished to give our good ship an undeserved slap in the face.

I left Radley's excellent hotel at Southampton on Monday morning, May 18th; the tender being announced in waiting to take off passengers to the Royal Mail steamer *Nile*. I was curious to see who were to be my companions for the next eighteen days; the little tender was crowded, but amidst visitors, friends of the departing, and officials, it was difficult to select the "outward bound." The perpetual north-east wind still blew off the land, but the water was like glass. Opposite to beautiful Netley the *Nile* was moored; a grand-looking two-masted steamer, high out of the water.

Confusion reigned on board. Passengers rushing to and fro in quest of their luggage; then inquiring for their cabins. "This chair for the deck," says one; "Those bags for my berth," says another; "Oh! beg pardon; I have got into the wrong cabin;" "I don't see my white umbrella," &c. An anxious mother counted over her children—one was missing. "Where's Gustavus? He came on board, I know." The black nurse went off in search; the little fellow had only strayed to the saloon, not dropped into the water like the bargee's son in "Jacob Faithful." You remember the imperturbable father's remark when a splash had been heard; he merely observed, taking the pipe out of his mouth, "I shouldn't wonder if it wasn't our Joe!"

The hands on board were most civil and attentive. Bayly, the steward of my cabin, quickly presented himself, and my numerous packages were safely stowed away. Then we repaired to

the saloon, the first sight of which was striking—
I may say dazzling. A succession of tables
extends, in two rows, three-fourths of its length;
they were arranged for a cold collation, with
vases of flowers at intervals; and suspended from
a bright metal bar are mahogany circulars—recep-
tacles for bottles and glasses—like elevated dumb-
waiters; a swinging white-metalled moderator is
supplied to each divisional table; the *tout-ensemble*
has a very pretty effect. Unlimited luncheon was
supplied gratuitously to all comers, but liquors
are to be procured only on a passenger's written
order, for which a card with the number of the
berth is presented by a steward. At 2.30 the
tender had returned with the mails—more than
250 great bags. How many anxious minds and
busy hands had been at work! Some time was
consumed in stowing them away in the hold, a
ship's officer superintending all the while. Then
the bell rang for the departure of visitors; and
now came the *tender* adieux. M—— had been so
useful. I leaned over the taffrail, and we waved
to one another till out of sight. I shall have
passed over some nine thousand miles of sea
before we meet again.

We are under weigh, and I am actually bound
for the West Indies; I can scarcely believe it. I

go below and arrange my cabin; there is plenty of room, for I have two berths and a sofa all to myself. I see Hurst Castle from the port-hole, its wide embrasures looking like great eyes watching the passers-by. At 5 o'clock we dine, and have an excellent repast. M——'s hint to bespeak my place at table was useful, for it is retained during the voyage. I found my card opposite to the Captain, and to him I was indebted for much of my enjoyment of the voyage. My neighbour on my left and I exchanged cards, and thus introduced ourselves; he was Mr. C——, of Barbadoes, and I should be pleased to think that my society was half as agreeable to him as his was to me. We fraternised at once, and I parted from him with regret. How often acquaintances formed in out-of-the-way places appear the pleasantest! Did any one ever return from a continental tour without having encountered "the nicest people possible?"

The evening was so calm and bright and mild; no movement but the vibration of the screw; we talked and smoked on deck till we were tired; then I read the last *Times* in the saloon till the extinction of the lights at 11 o'clock drove me to my berth, where I found I could sleep as soundly as upon land.

CHAPTER II.

OUR PASSENGERS.

It takes some time to settle down to this new mode of life. One cannot at first divest one's self of the idea that the post must come, and the newspaper to accompany the matutinal cup of tea.

There is a good deal of rolling to-day, and the tables in the saloon are covered with "fiddles," as they are called, wooden frames dividing the tables into compartments, so as to restrain within convenient limits the eccentric deviations of plates and the other paraphernalia of eating and drinking. But this contrivance was not always successful, for on one occasion at dinner—like "a vaulting ambition, which o'erleaps itself"—an unusual roll sent the soup-plates with their contents into the laps of the occupants of one side of the tables, to the manifest discomfort of the gentlemen, and the dismay of ladies who wore silk dresses.

The discipline of this ship seems admirable. Everything goes on like clockwork; at the first stroke of the ship's bell, a hand-bell is rung through the main-deck, and the tables are all ready for the passengers. My day is thus divided: at 6 A.M. Bayly brings a large cup of excellent tea and slices of bread-and-butter to my cabin; I then rise and take a cold sea-water bath—there is a bath-room on each side of the vessel; at 8 o'clock he brings hot water, and I dress; at 9 breakfast. An abundant meal is provided: fresh bread every morning; the milk, I fancy, is condensed, and the eggs preserved, although we have cows and hens on board. I append some of our *menus* to show how we fare:—

BILL OF FARE.
BREAKFAST.

Grilled Steak.   Mutton Chops.   Curried Rice.
Savoury Omelets.   Deviled Bones.   Sausages.   Haddocks.
Mashed Potatoes.   Grilled Ham.

JNO. MITCHELL, *Purser.*

Dated *May 23rd*, 1874.

BILL OF FARE.
BREAKFAST.

Grilled Ham.   Sausages.   Curried Rice.
Salt Fish and Egg Sauce.   Omelets.   Deviled Bones.
Mutton Chops.   Haddocks.   Herrings.   Potatoes.

JNO. MITCHELL, *Purser.*

Dated *May 25th*, 1874.

After breakfast there is a general smoke and talk, either on the spar-deck, or (which is more popular) the port gangway on the main-deck, where there are large gratings admitting plenty of air, and where the weather can be excluded with shutters if it be unfavourable.

When 12 o'clock (mid-day) is reported to the Captain, the run that the ship has made during the last twenty-four hours is posted at the head of the companion. There is always a little excitement about this; one is glad to get up any sort of excitement at sea; sometimes lotteries are arranged, the person who draws the number nearest to the advertised speed winning the pool.

At 12.30 the bell summons us to luncheon, at which sardines, cold meats, cheese, cake, buns, and fruit play their part. The children and servants have their dinner in the saloon at 1 o'clock. At 4.30 the bell rings to announce the half-hour before dinner. It is not the custom to dress for it, although some English ladies do, we islanders are so national; but the warning gives an opportunity for a refreshing of one's self with soap and water, and also for little *réunions* before the bar, where one is invited to join in a drink after the American fashion; and it is not considered polite to refuse. I am not aware that many breaches of decorum occurred in this respect. I give you two specimens of *comestibles* provided at this important meal, regarded on board ship, and often on land, as *the* event of the day. I may add, that the wines are good, and the prices moderate; they, as well as the food, are supplied by the Company.

BILL OF FARE.

Soups.—Julienne and Pea.
Fish.—Turbot and Anchovy Sauce.
Entrées.—Haricot Mutton, Bœuf aux Olives.
Boiled Joint.—Chicken and Bath Chaps.
Roast Joint.—Beef.
Salad.—Lettuce.
Vegetables.—Mashed and Baked Potatoes, Caravances.
Curry and Rice.—Fowl.
Pastry.—Cabinet Pudding, Apple Puffs.
Dessert.—Apples, Figs, Walnuts, Olives, Dates, Filberts.

JNO. MITCHELL, *Purser.*

Dated *May 19th*, 1874.

BILL OF FARE.

Soups.—Macaroni and Ox Tail.
Fish.—Fried Cod and Anchovy Sauce.
Entrées.—Haricot Mutton, Roast Ducks and Green Peas, Rump Steak Puddings.
Roast Joint.—Beef.
Salad.—Lettuce.
Vegetables.—Mashed and Baked Potatoes, Forced Onions.
Curry and Rice.—Mutton.
Pastry.—Plum Pudding, Lemon Jellies, Custards.
Dessert.—Almonds, Raisins, Walnuts, Figs, Dates, Grapes.

JNO. MITCHELL, *Purser.*

Dated *May 21st*, 1874.

At 8.30 the summons to tea is rung out, when tea and coffee, preserves and fruits, are laid on the table. This is the last meal of the day, but, if later, sandwiches or biscuits are asked for, they are always forthcoming. In the evening there is the walk on deck; below, the tables are cleared, and parties are formed for cards, or draughts, or chess. The love of gambling is very strong among the Spaniards, and they were very noisy over their games.

We have now passed beyond the swell of the Bay of Biscay, the sea is unruffled, the sky speckless, and the temperature delightful, about 75°. The fiddles are removed from the tables; the awning is spread over the after-deck, and new faces seem to appear daily. One lady pertinaciously remained below until she reached her destination; the stewardess said that "she would not make an effort." Now lighter clothing is agreeable; greatcoats and rugs are piled away, and make one uncomfortable to contemplate, and the ports and doors of cabins are kept carefully open. A poor pigeon that had attended us from the Channel, resting sometimes on the rigging, has disappeared to-day; exhausted, probably, from want of food. Pigeons seldom make mistakes. I wonder what its intentions were?

We have very few passengers, only forty-two in the saloon; for the most part residents returning to the West Indies, some to Central America. A merry-hearted Dutch girl is going to Surinam to her husband,

"Γυναικα τ'ου γυναικα,"

having been married by proxy in her own country. A curious arrangement. Does the other contracting party go through the same form in his? She had originally embarked on board a Dutch steamer, but the engines breaking down, the vessel had to put into Oporto. The young vrow had then to take ship to Southampton, and so joined the *Nile*. She had been already ten weeks at sea, but was one of the liveliest of our passengers. Her ringing voice was heard above others at all hours of the day. She speaks English, French, and German, and we were always glad to converse with her when we had a chance; but a compatriot of hers, the attorney-general proceeding to the same colony, pretty well engrossed her attention, and as I believe he was not the proxy, we thought it unfair. Then there were a brother and sister, very young Spaniards; she looked about fourteen, and had been six years at a school at Largs, N.B. They are going to their parents at St. Juan Nicaragua.

There are several lads who are returning home after education has been, it is supposed, completed in England or elsewhere. They are a restless set—great bores I may say, always in exercise, hopping matches, or gymnasticizing on ropes, or playing at bull. This is a favourite pastime on board ship. A square black board, on inclined plane, with numbers and zeros in squares, painted white, is placed on the deck; the game consists in pitching from a certain distance circular discs of lead sewn up in leather on the numbers.

A little urchin of thirteen years or so—a sharp mulatto boy—was continually playing tricks, and was frequently chased round the decks—a great nuisance. "You shall catch it," was often exclaimed, but he did not, for he was never caught. One night, however, he did catch it. His custom of a night was, when all was still, to prowl about the passages attired in ghostly attire—a "winding sheet" from his berth. He would knock at cabin-doors, and when the inmates appeared they were startled at the apparition, which met them with upstretched arms, and then rapidly disappeared. At one midnight hour a wary passenger lay in wait, and emerging noiselessly behind the ghost, administered such a spat on his back with the flat of a razor-strop, that the scapegrace with a scream gave up the ghost, fleeing precipitately, and minus his assumed garment.

There is a lady on board—a Genoëse—not bad-looking, with a pale complexion, and expressive dark eyes, going out to join her husband in Guatemala. She sits on deck in a brown-holland dress, from, I believe, daybreak to sunset, with scarcely any intermission. She is of pleasant demeanour when addressed, and speaks gracefully, as most Italians do; but her conversation is confined to her own intellectual gifts, the noble descent of her husband's family, and admiration of the poets of her country. Poor thing! Her intellectual gifts are certainly high-flown, if not flown away altogether. Her husband does not seem to have supported the honours of his ancient pedigree, having become bankrupt on no very creditable terms, so far as I could make out; and *au reste* she is undeniably prosy. And yet there is something interesting and attractive about her. Monsieur C—— tried to make himself acceptable to her for some time, and took the trouble of preferring some requests of hers to the purser; but he afterwards ceased his attentions, for she told him he resembled Mephistopheles; and so he maintains that she has *une araignée au plafond*. There is no doubt she has "a bee in her bonnet." I understand that she eats very little, and that little in her cabin. I asked her why she did not attend the meals in the saloon. It was on account of the bad manners of those who sat near her. She accepted a seat at the Captain's table once, but some gentlemen ate too much, and she did not appear there again. She complained of the heat of her cabin; one morning she was indignant. "Conceive the villainy," she said to me; "they have placed a hot man in a cabin on each side of me!" I think the Captain and I were her chief comforters, the Captain certainly, for he is every one's, a favourite with all, especially the ladies. A chat with him is a thing looked out for, and the lady who contemplates exercise on deck, hopes that his arm may be proffered.

There are several Spanish-speaking passengers bound for various parts; but with few exceptions they are not a very good lot, and, as they seldom know any language but their own, their society is pretty well restricted to themselves. We have one genuine Yankee. He hails from San Francisco, where he was raised, I believe, and like the generality of his countrymen is quaint in his diction, and amusing in his remarks; he is a pleasant companion and an observant man of the world. He has been travelling for ten months for the benefit of his health; he is always ready for anything, be it cocktail, bull, walk, talk, smoke, *écarté*, or whist. Among the miscellaneous I may include a young black, whose presence might be objected to on several accounts, as he was forward, pushing, with a loud harsh voice, and "irrepressible," which I found to be the characteristic of gentlemen of colour. The Yankee and he had a disagreement on deck one night. The Darkey, heated with a succession of "drinks," rushed down franticly into the saloon, exclaiming to the stewards, "Give me a knife, a knife, I say! I have been insulted and will revenge myself;" of course the murderous means were not supplied, and he returned on deck, where some further altercation ensued. Next morning Mr. D—— received a note to this effect: "Dear Sir, having been grossly insulted by you last night, I demand that satisfaction which one gentleman, &c. I, therefore, invite you, if you are not a coward, to land with me at St. Thomas's, and meet me with a friend at a convenient place, which I can point out, in single combat, and as I have the right to choose the weapons, I name swords. Yours, &c."

On receipt of this, Mr. D—— consulted Mr. C—— as to what he ought to do. "Knock him down," said Mr. C—— in his haste. The other, however, objected, and properly, to this violent course, as he was on board a British vessel, and should be putting himself in the wrong. "Well then, throw the letter in his face, and tell him to write no more nonsense to you; and that if he attacks you, you will be prepared to defend yourself." This course was adopted. A San Franciscan was not likely to be unprovided with a revolver, nor with knowledge of its use. Cooler moments brought peaceful sentiments, and I saw them enjoying a sherry-cobbler together before dinner.

Mr. C—— had been amusing us the day before with a narration of practical jokes which had been perpetrated some while ago in Barbadoes. Amongst these was a duel forced upon two would-be non-combatants with scarcely any cause of disagreement, the one a Frenchman just arrived, the other an Englishman. This latter, when the hostile meeting had been arranged, was made privy to the joke, and consented to fall on the first discharge, the pistols, of course, not having been loaded with ball. A medical man (or a pseudo one) was in attendance, and everything complete. The ground was carefully measured, and the principals were then told by their seconds to turn round and fire. Down fell the Englishman. The pretended friends of the Frenchman hurried him off to a place of concealment, in order to avoid the fatal penalty he had incurred by violating the laws of the island. A coffin, supposed to contain the remains of his antagonist, was, to his horror, ostentatiously borne past the windows of his retreat; a policeman arrived with a warrant to attach his person, but he was smuggled off by the back-door to a steamer just leaving; was never seen again, and probably still lives in the belief that he has shed man's blood. It occurred to us afterwards that we had missed an opportunity of casting ridicule on the Darkey's affair, by insisting that the mortal combat should take place so soon as the saloon was clear, when two of the ship's cutlasses should be provided for the occasion. But I shall weary you with these details; at sea, amidst so much inevitable listless idleness, trifles such as these, *faute de mieux*, have an amusing importance, but scarcely bear reporting. I shall therefore introduce the other passengers incidentally. I cannot, however, refrain from recording the interest I took in the conversation of a venerable clergyman.

Although so unobtrusive and simple-hearted, I think he would not object to my naming him, *honoris causâ*, Dr. Phillips. At the age of seventy-two he is returning to George Town, Demerara, with his son-in-law, a hard-working young clergyman, married to his only daughter. Having previously come out on a visit to them, he had found his health so greatly improved by the equable temperature of Demerara, that he had given up a living in England, and a residence at Torquay, and had settled himself in that genial climate, he thought, for the rest of his days. The Doctor was one of the most pertinacious walkers on board, and his perambulations on deck, when he was discoursing on some favourite topic, were sufficient to tax the lungs and legs of even an active companion. His conversation had an additional interest for me, as he had lived a good deal at B——, several years ago, and could recall the names of many persons I had known in my youth, almost all long passed away. So that with the novelty of this mode of life—the number of new characters of all countries (and there is always an effort made to be mutually acceptable with fresh acquaintances), withal the feeling of getting daily stronger in health, counteracts much of the tedium of being in "a prison with the chance of being drowned," and so in enjoyable repose not yet monotonous,

> " Le temps s'en va,
> Le temps s'en va, ma belle,
> Las le temps non, mais nous,
> Nous en allons."

CHAPTER III.

OUR SHIP.

You remember Xavier de Maistre's amusing *Voyage autour de ma Chambre*. Well, I made an excursion to-day round "the house of my pilgrimage," in company with one of the ship's officers who kindly offered his services. Besides the Captain (who, by the way, is Commodore, senior officer, of the Company's fleet) there are five officers, distinguishable by the number of gold stripes on their sleeves, also a surgeon, purser, and assistant purser. The first officer takes the active management of the ship, the second has charge of the mails in addition to his other duties. The officers mess together, except the purser and surgeon, who take their meals with the passengers in the saloon. Their messing is found by the Company, and 1s. 6d. *per diem* allowed to each officer for wine. At Southampton there is a club-house for all the Company's officers who may be on shore, maintained at the Company's expense with a small deduction from each officer's pay.

The *Nile* is all iron, 376 feet long, and 40 broad; her depth 38 feet, whole tonnage 2,994, registered tonnage 1,642, horse-power 600. She can hold 1,040 tons of coals, her daily average consumption of which is 40. She is four years old, was built by Day and Summers, of Southampton, and cost £100,000. She is brig-rigged, and carries a large amount of canvas. She has a flush deck, and is steered from the bridge, but there is also a steering apparatus abaft. The deck is scrubbed every morning. I may mention that a notice-board on the after-deck requests the passengers not to expectorate on the decks, a request to which our shipmates the Spaniards paid little attention. It is expressed in English, French, and Spanish:—

"Se supplica à los Señores Passageros de no es capir sobre la Cubierta di Popa."

I quote this one because it struck me that *popa* is the immediate source of our word poop; so many of our sea terms come to us through the Spanish, and *popa* doubtless is derived from the Latin *puppis*. The Captain's cabin and the ship's company's cook-house are on deck.

Aft on the main-deck (that is below, you will

understand, there is the saloon, 101 feet long, with sofas round the stern part, and tables for reading and writing; the rest is appropriated to the dining-tables. These tables are flanked by cabins, which, I believe, have been a subsequent introduction; this part of the saloon consequently is narrower than the stern end. In the centre, dividing the two rows of tables, is a longitudinal opening for the purpose of affording light and air to the cabins on the lower deck. A liquor bar on one side, and a pantry on the other, complete this division, with a wide companion leading up to the spar-deck. Emerging from the saloon, on either side there is a gangway with a grating (this was the favourite resort of a coterie of Spanish ladies), then a long passage with cabins on the out-board; the centre is engrossed by the kitchen, bakery, and engines; in the middle of each of these long passages there is a bath-room fitted with a marble bath. Beyond these passages you arrive at another division with cabins on each side, and a wide space in the middle with tables and seats. Down the centre there is an opening to the lower deck, similar to that in the saloon. At the end of this row of cabins there is another gangway, opening out to the seaboard at either end, where one's chair may be stationed with advantage.

These are the best cabins, "main-deck outside" (as they are described in the Company's little hand-book), and are worth the extra charge. They are larger, cooler, quieter, and removed from the turmoil and traffic and heat of the engines and offices. I advise those who are going to the "Far West" to secure a berth in this division, and in case of there being a small number of passengers, an individual may be fortunate enough to obtain a cabin to himself, as was my case. The second-best cabins are in the long passages, the port side being preferable, as being clear of the traffic to the kitchen and its accessories. The next are in the saloon. Those on the lower deck are dark and close, as the ports can seldom be opened there. It is well to bring a chair on board; one of those light ones that shut up close is most convenient, for although there are, of course, benches on deck, a seat may not always be easily procured if there are many passengers; moreover, it is pleasant to sit where you choose. I will avoid minor details, as neither you nor I are seafaring people. I will add that the cost of a berth in the best position (main-deck outside) for a single voyage to Jamaica is £43 10s.: this includes everything but liquors. The stewards expect a gratuity, which they well deserve, for they have a fatiguing life of it, being in requisition, with some reliefs, from 5 A.M. to 11 P.M. Those who have charge of cabins are better paid, and your comforts are much enhanced by their attentions; but the saloon waiters seldom, I fancy, receive much extra remuneration, and their wages are only £30 *per annum*, with board, of course. These men commence scrubbing the main-deck every morning at about four or five o'clock. On a return ticket there is an abatement of 25 *per cent.*, available for twelve calendar months; my passage consequently cost £65 5*s*. There is also a reduction in the charge in the case of families and children. If a life be insured, notice must be given at the offices; in my case one office liberally made no surcharge, provided I did not remain over one month at Jamaica; another charged me 5 *per cent.* on the premium for the permission.

A large clothes-bag for worn linen is essential; a voyage of eighteen days requiring a goodly stock, this bag shortly acquires very protuberant expansion, and as it is not convenient to be banged on the head by it every time you pass your cabin door, it may be a relief to some minds, as it was to mine, to find that linen could be washed on board for fourpence a piece. The ship's company's cook was the laundry-man, but whether, like "the poor 'Vorkus boy," it "was boiled in the soup," I cannot say, but its colour was not pearly, and he certainly was not an adept at "getting up fine linen."

We brought out on the fore-part of the deck fifty-eight sheep, eight pigs, one horse, and cocks and hens and other poultry innumerable. The horse was going to Demerara; the cost of his passage was £25; then there is the use of a horse-box, which costs £5, and provender for the voyage £2. The crowing and cackling were deafening at first, but as we ate them off, by a wise provision of nature, the noise sensibly diminished.

Whit-Sunday, 24th May. — I am sleepy this morning, for I have had a disturbed night. It came on to blow—a sudden squall, I fancy—and I was awoke by being nearly rolled out of my berth; it was just before midnight, for soon after I heard eight bells. I am getting nautical, you perceive. There was such running about overhead, and boatswain's whistles—furling sails, I presume, for a great deal of canvas has been displayed all day. Screeching noises everywhere; the vessel seemed compressed and crushed as though she were a mighty clothes-basket being squeezed; and some sounds for which I could not account at the time, resembled the cracking of hundreds of whips. Surely they were not "flogging the engine." I discovered afterwards that it was the flapping of the halyards and cordage.

At daybreak—I could not long have closed my eyes—I was startled again. My cabin is amidships, abreast of the engine-room. A creaking crank with a rattling chain was hard at work in raising the cinders to the upper deck, in order to be thrown overboard. The next operation is to discharge the accumulation of brine from the engines. The full force of the steam is turned on to get rid of this through a scupper, and out it comes, hissing, spouting, roaring—oh! a delectable noise: it must be heard to be appreciated. This fortunately does not last long, but then begin holy-stoning, and scrubbing the decks; and this is the day of rest! I peered out of my cabin at 4 o'clock, and saw the boot-cleaners already at work. At last I was exhausted. At 6 o'clock when Bayly roused me, I was sound asleep. He tells me it is a beautiful morning, and very warm. I speak to him about changing my cabin, and he says it can be done.

This is somebody's birthday, and I do not forget it. I have not altered my watch, which is now one hour and forty minutes in advance of the ship's time; and I often consult it, picturing to myself what dear ones are doing at home. At

10.30 we have Divine Service. At the ringing of the bell the entire ship's company is mustered round the after-deck. Stewards in blue jackets, cooks in white, seamen in jerseys, with *Nile* across them —all look very clean and respectable. One hundred and twenty-eight all told. The Captain goes round, and the purser calls over the roll, at which each man in turn touches his cap. Then the order is given "Below," and they rattle down the companion, and take up the best seats in the saloon. The officers followed, then the passengers, and sat at the tables. Dear old Dr. Phillips, in surplice, stole, and hood, read the prayers solemnly and in an audible voice; Mr. Fox reading the lessons. After which the latter, who was not in canonicals, delivered a short, impressive, and appropriate sermon, which he commenced by saying he did by kind permission of the Captain. He took his text from Mark v. 38 : " Carest thou not that we perish ?" He remarked that this incident is repeated three times in the New Testament, but very differently told. He hoped that in tribulation we should feel confidence in addressing our prayers to Him who is a God of love ; but not in the tone in which the disciples addressed their Master in the storm.

The weather is again as fine as can be—not

sultry; the thermometer 72°, sitting out on deck under the awning is very enjoyable. Patches of light yellow-coloured weed drift past, which I am told are "gulf weed," and which I see noticed by Canon Kingsley in his "At Last;" a work in which his profound love of nature and its history invests with a charm and an interest objects otherwise unnoticed by the *profanum vulgus.* It appears that this gulf weed has nothing to do with the gulf-stream. A passenger tells me he saw a nautilus sailing by; I am sorry that I did not. The only specimens of animal life that I have seen off the ship are a couple of Mother Carey's chickens, which the Captain pointed out to me. Next day, however, I could not say this, for I had my first view of live flying fish. I could scarcely believe at first that they were fish, they flew so like birds, like large sea-swallows. I went to the bows to have a better sight of them, and while I was staring there, one of the crew took the opportunity of chalking my shoe, an operation performed upon a novice for the purpose of obtaining a "drink your health." However, the paying your footing is a mild ordeal in comparison with Neptune's shaving, which one hears of as practised on those who crossed the Line for the first time; so that

I was glad to be mulcted in a small gratuity, especially as the men are very well behaved, and always civil when asked stupid questions by ignorant landsmen.

A fine-looking tall Negress of benevolent aspect is often parading on deck a white baby, of which she appears very fond. It appears she went out as nurse of a child to England, and she is now returning, having adopted this baby, which had been abandoned by its parents. There was some obscurity in her statement, upon which she did not seem disposed to throw light. But some of my fellow-passengers who are supposed to know more about the matter, said that this was a very good woman, and deserved encouragement; and they promoted a subscription, to which we all contributed, towards enabling her to buy a cow, which would afford her sufficient means of subsistence at home. If so, it is cheap living there: £7 10s. was collected.

A passenger proceeding to Lima, in conversation one day complained to me of suffering from nausea. I asked if he had tried "Pyretic Saline." He had never heard of it. I offered to give him a dose, which he accepted. By the way, it occurs to me how fond people are of prescribing for others; there is always a great liberality in offering remedies, not often accepted. I have known a man who would give you a hat-box full of pills, but would hesitate to advance a penny stamp. However, the sick man told me next day he felt already better; "would I let him have another dose?" so I lent him the bottle. Most of the passengers were provided with this preparation, and I found that in Jamaica and elsewhere it was in extensive use. He now came to tell me that I had made him a different man; and in gratitude he had written out a remedy for rheumatism, which had been given to him by a learned man in the north of England, and which he and some of his friends had personally tested and found most wonderfully efficacious. It is so curious, that I transcribe it for your edification.

"Take common worms, such as are used as baits in angling; wash and clean them in several waters, and after drying them with a cloth, half fill a champagne bottle with them; bury it three feet under the ground, cork downwards, and let it remain for three months; then take up and strain off the juice, and apply to the parts affected three times a day: to be rubbed briskly on the skin."

He explained that if the bottle were filled it

would probably explode; so great is the force of the gas generated, that when he was drawing the cork of an exhumed bottle, it flew out and hit him in the eye; and that a champagne bottle was preferable, as being the strongest. I thanked him, and expressed my regret that if I should have a sudden seizure on board, the means of preparing his remedy would not now be at hand.

I have had a long talk with a fine-looking and intelligent Colour-sergeant of the 3rd Battalion Grenadier Guards; he has been fifteen years in the service; fourteen of these as a non-commissioned officer. He is going out as Regimental Sergeant-major of the 2nd West India Regiment. He has a wife and three children on board. We had a discussion as to what I fear will prove a serious and increasing difficulty; namely, the recruitment of the army. "The pay must be raised," said he, "or the men won't be got."*

Next morning after breakfast, I had the satisfaction of finding all my worldly goods shifted into one of the best forward cabins on the starboard

* The Council of the Royal United Service Institution has decided to give a gold medal annually for the best essay on a naval or military subject, and I am glad to find that the subject of the first is to be:—
"The best mode of providing recruits and forming reserves for the British army."

side. It is calculated to accommodate three passengers. The chief officers and the assistant pursers are the only ones between me and the gangway. I am very comfortable here; my only wish is for a table to write at, but a reasonable compromise is effected by placing a deal box on the sofa.

One day the ship's company was exercised at "Fire quarters." Every man has his station; at the sound of the fire-bell, each steward seizes a blanket off the first berth and rushes to his place; the cooks—I don't know what they are bound to bring—but they were all present. Then we had "Man overboard," and the quarter-boats were manned and ready to be lowered with rapid precision. Such is life on board.

CHAPTER IV.

LAND AT LAST.

Wednesday, May 27th.—I arose to bathe before 6 o'clock, and looked out of the port (which is now kept open all night), and saw that it was raining heavily; but the weather cleared up after breakfast, and the sun made up for the temporary eclipse by shining upon us with additional vigour.

As we are proceeding to the land of the sugar-cane, and carrying out many persons interested in its culture, you may suppose that I hear repeated discussions on this subject. One gentleman asserts that the cost of production of sugar is 1½*d*. per lb., and that, as it is retailed in London and elsewhere at 3*d*. per lb., the sale of it at this price offers no margin for profit. This is certainly a gloomy view of the matter; for, in the face of so much competition, the price of the commodity is more likely to fall than to rise. Another speaker observed that it was a well-known fact that the retailers, *i.e.* the grocers, never expect a profit on it, but sell it in order to attract customers to their other goods. Attention was directed to an article in *Public Opinion* for May 16, 1874, which one of the parties to the discussion produced for general edification. In an article headed "Sugar Refining," purporting to be a report of a paper recently read on the above subject at the Society of Arts, by Dr. Griffin, it is stated that brown sugar is in general unfit for human consumption. The writer considers raw sugar decidedly objectionable, unless it be of the very finest quality, and quotes an authority to show that colonies of insects are found in it—a most obnoxious impurity if the statement be correct, for it is not destroyed even by hot water, and burrows under the skin like the itch-insect. It was found in 78 out of 83 samples of sugar purchased in London. An instance was cited where Dr. C—— calculated that a sample of the sugar supplied to one of the Workhouses of Dublin contained at least 100,000 insects to the pound, and that the process of refining without blood or lime, as employed by Messrs. Finzell at their refinery at Counterslip, was the most free from animalcules that had as yet been brought under his notice.

Here is comfort for the consumer! If it become

generally known and believed, every one will be growing thin by abstinence from sugar, on the Banting system! The above article is a capital advertisement, but I did not perceive that the speakers entertained any pious horror in swallowing this prolific animalcule; but what they do consider the great enemy of the proprietor of sugar estates is the producer of beet-root sugar. He is the arch-fiend whom they would gladly see destroyed by "the itch-like insect," or any other subtle process.

There are several Trinidadians on board, and I hear naturally a good deal about their island. How little the general public knows about the West Indies! I am one of the general public. We have a resident proprietor on board, whose name refers to Italian descent, and his resemblance to the late Emperor Napoleon impressed us all; he is consul to the kingdom of Italy, and seeing that I was an inquirer, good-naturedly lent me his printed report on the island, addressed to the Italian Minister of Foreign Affairs. I shall spare you the results of my perusal of the consular *brochure*, because Canon Kingsley, in his charming "At Last," has done ample justice to the natural graces of this beautiful island. He passed seven weeks there in the winter of 1869-70, and his graphic descriptions make one long to tread amidst the entanglements of "primeval forests," to step on that wondrous "Pitch Lake," and to gaze upon the gigantic vegetation of this favoured region. I merely add that Trinidad is the largest and southernmost of the Lesser Antilles, and, next to Jamaica, is the largest of the British West India Islands. It is 48 miles long, and 35 broad. It contains 1,755 square miles, or 1,122,880 acres; of these latter (in 1866) 68,592, or about 1-16th of the whole, only were cultivated. This, I understood, arose from the high price set upon land, the Government wishing to discourage small occupiers.

Trinidad originally belonged to Spain; it possesses the curious and probably unique circumstance of a French-speaking population in an island which never belonged to France. This arose from the immigration of French residents from Granada, St. Vincent's, St. Lucia, and Dominica, in dread of English domination, when those islands came into the possession of England; and subsequently from the political troubles caused by the outbreak of the 'French revolution and the massacres at St. Domingo. Its population in 1783 consisted only of 126 whites, 295 free men of colour, 310 slaves, and 2,032 *indigènes*, total 2,763.

In 1790 the population had increased to 10,422, and in 1797 to 17,718; in this year the island was captured by the British, in whose possession it has remained ever since. In 1866 the population amounted to 85,000. The capital of the island is Port of Spain, with a population of (at that date) 20,000 souls. The fertility of the land is remarkable, and the exports consist chiefly of sugar, rum, cocoa, coffee, and cotton. Its geographical position is one of great importance, both in a commercial and political point of view. Its magnificent Gulf of Paria is sufficient to shelter the navies of the world, whilst its proximity to the delta of the Orinoco entitles it to become the entrepôt of the commerce of the south; whilst as a military basis it commands the Orinoco—that vast artery which leads to the very heart of the Spanish American republics.

The tropical nights are so beautiful, warm, windless, cloudless; the sky studded with stars innumerable, which shine so much more brightly in this clear atmosphere. Down in my cabin, before consigning myself to rest, I look out of the open port and watch the water as it rushes past. The vessel glides along so statelily, and, for'ard as I am, I can see the wave, raised and cleft by her stem, beaten off and flying, as it were, from its gigantic antagonist in shattered scud, white as reefs of untrodden snow, dispersing itself at last into fantastic reticulations, like delicate tracery of Mechlin lace, sparkling with phosphorescence.

Sunday, the last day of the month, which made its early appearance in tears, dropping just enough water, as we jocosely remark, to lay the dust; but smiles succeed, and all is bright—*post nubila Phœbus.*

I have now been fourteen days at sea, and I must confess that this *nil nisi pontus et aer* becomes very monotonous. Despite pleasant companionship, it is wearisome; I have talked myself out, and my associates have done the same. Fine opportunity for reading and meditation, you would say (not for writing, that is under difficulties), but the sea air makes one so drowsy that I cannot succeed in either; it is generally understood on board that "reading in your cabin" is synonymous with "sleeping." The same daily routine, without any variety. I may exclaim with the Psalmist, "One day telleth another: and one night certifieth another."

We expect to reach Barbadoes to-night. What a relief it will be to see land again!

No Divine Service to-day; crew engaged in getting out luggage and merchandise. I took a long walk with Dr. Phillips, and this is a final one in all human probability. He is so pleased to revive recollections of B—— days; and then we fall, as usual, into theology.

This is the last dinner, too, together with many of us, for here passengers proceeding to Demerara, Trinidad, Martinique, Dominica, Guadaloupe, Antigua, and St. Kitts, are transferred to one of the Company's "intercolonial steamers." The mail steamers that leave Southampton on the 17th of the month proceed to Barbadoes direct, whilst those on the 2nd of the month proceed to St. Thomas's, and there transfer their mails and passengers for the Gulf of Mexico and the islands route.

We had champagne to celebrate the occasion. There are several leaving us here, the loss of whose society I shall much regret; the acquaintance seems not of fourteen days, but of as many years. And now our healths are drunk, the friendly chat at table is over, and we are on deck, for Barbadoes is looming in the distance. Telescopes and binoculars are produced; some cluster on the bows in order to enjoy a nearer sight; all are straining their eyes towards the island. There is the lighthouse, and now we are running under the land. A white light is displayed on shore, then a rocket is fired, and answered from the ship; then another and another. There is quite an excitement on board, and on shore doubtless the arrival of the Royal Mail from England is a stirring event. The glare of a blue-light displays to us the masts of many ships; we are in the midst of them; the engines are stopped, the chain cable rattles through the hawse-hole, and we anchor in Carlisle Bay. This is my first sight of land in the New World.

In consequence of the greater rarity of the atmosphere, the evenings in these latitudes close more quickly than in ours; as soon as the sun sets it is dark night. Half-past seven o'clock of a summer evening, the hour of our anchoring, would not be dark with us, but it was so here. But such a night! The heavens glittered with stars, and among them I beheld, for the first time, the Southern Cross. Accustomed as we Christians are to regard the cross as the solemn symbol of our faith, one cannot see this remarkable constellation—certainly at first—without some sentiments allied to veneration. Other stars were pointed out, of the names of which I had hitherto been in ignorance. The water was like glass reflecting the lights, for there was scarcely a breath of wind.

The scene around was dazzling and confusing, the rekindling of life after inanimate monotony of the sea. The moon is shining brightly, and the lights on shore and on the vessels have a pretty effect. Some one said it was like a Dutch sea-piece; it does remind me of a Vandervelde. Now shore-boats are rowed alongside by black men in white shirts and trousers, and there is such tusseling and strife, each being eager to get his boat in first. As they chatter and vociferate you can see the whites of their eyes and their teeth. Visitors come on board to claim wives or friends. I am actually inquired for by name. Who can know me here? A letter for me, addressed on board R.M.S.S. at St. Thomas's, and so brought on here by the Company's agent. I thanked the bearer, and rushed to the saloon to read it. It was from F——, to welcome me to Jamaica, with a lady's P.S., "Bring plenty of Tauchnitz volumes from St. Thomas's."

On deck again, I am introduced to several of the residents; most cordial is their demeanour. Mr. C—— pressed me to be a guest at his house, but the only hospitality which I was able to accept was an invitation to dine on my return. As the Captain was also included, I considered the acceptance confirmed. Barbadoes is called "Bimshire," and the residents "Bims." Why I don't know; I suppose I shall be made aware before long. I can only say, from my very short experience, that I should have considered it a more appropriate designation if this "tight little island" had been numbered among one of the "Friendly" or "Society" Islands.

As it was Sunday, and every establishment was closed, moreover, as it was dark, I did not land. The mails were hoisted out, but it was half an hour past midnight before the deafening clanking of the steam-crane had ceased to discharge the Barbadian cargo; then the *Nile* got under weigh, and I retired to rest.

CHAPTER V.

ALONG THE ISLANDS.

Monday, June 1st.—The saloon has quite a melancholy appearance, owing to the absence of so many cheerful faces. Few tables are now required; ours would have been well-nigh denuded, but for the accession of two English gentlemen who had joined the steamer for passage to Jamaica.

We are passing St. Lucia on the port side, but it is so bathed in mist, that we can scarcely distinguish the outline. I could just make out a huge eminence soaring above the haze, which I fancy must be part of the chain of mountains which I see in the map extends longitudinally through the centre of the island. In the French Antilles, mountains are commonly called *Mornes*, a name which they retain here. I was sorry not to be able to see more of this island, which is said to be one of the most beautiful of the whole group.*

---

* "Among all these beautiful islands, St. Lucia is, I think, the most beautiful."—*At Last*, p. 51.

Originally a French possession, it has been wrested by the British. Ceded by treaty, on the first declaration of war it became again and again the scene of sanguinary contests. Here fought and bled leaders well known to fame, Rodney, Hood, and Jervis. It was off Gros-ilet Bay that Rodney took up his station with thirty-six sail of the line, to watch the movements of the French fleet of thirty-four ships of the line and sixteen frigates, assembled in Port Royal Bay, Martinique, under Count de Grasse. The design of the enemy was to effect a junction with the Spanish fleet off St. Domingo, and then to proceed to a sweeping conquest of the whole of our sugar colonies from Barbadoes to Jamaica. And who can say what might have been the issue of a naval encounter with combined forces "amounting to near fifty ships of the line, and twenty thousand land troops?"* The honour of the British flag, the preservation of our West Indian colonies, our pre-eminence as a naval power, our very existence as an independent nation, were at stake. But the mighty project was defeated, and Britain's dominion on the ocean secured by the ability and courage of one man.

* See the account in Blane, who was present.—*Select Dissertations on Subjects of Medical Science.*

Here, on the 10th of April, 1794, H.R.H. the Prince Edward (father of our most gracious Queen), after a fatiguing march of fourteen hours, planted the British colours on Morne Fortuné, the chief fortress and eminence of St. Lucia. Here Moore, afterwards Sir John Moore of Corunna, Governor of the island, and the gallant Abercrombie, retained the conquest with all the tenacity of insular bulldogs. Guns were dragged across ravines, and up acclivities of mountains and rocks, by the zeal and labour of devoted soldiers and sailors. The result remains to us, we know not and care not how obtained. Their valorous deeds lie buried with them :—

> "The evil that men do lives after them ;
> The good is oft interred with their bones."

In a letter addressed to the Earl of Sandwich in May, 1778, Lord Rodney forcibly impressed upon that Minister the necessity of securing possession of St. Lucia: that he had once preferred Martinique, but that he was subsequently fully convinced that St. Lucia was more important of the two. "Martinique," he wrote, "though possessing four harbours, has none equal to the carénage of St. Lucia, or so secure and capable of being defended; where the largest ships-of-war can be careened, be secure during the hurricane months, and always ready to afford a speedy succour to His Majesty's other islands."*

The Government of the day so far adopted Rodney's suggestion, that a force was dispatched for the conquest of St. Lucia, which it effected, and the island has been retained by England; but it does not appear that its fine harbour has ever been utilised. Modern policy has adopted Bermuda as the principal strategical point in this direction, and I was informed that the defensive works for this naval anchorage will cost, when completed, £395,000.

At mid-day we came upon Martinique (or Martinico as it was formerly called), the largest of the Windward Islands: about forty-five miles long and sixteen wide. For a couple of hours we were steaming along its shores, with its diversified scenery of hill and dale, rocks and verdure. I could scarcely withdraw myself for a few minutes for luncheon from the position on the bridge which I was allowed to occupy. The island is of irregular form, indented by many bays; from the seaward it appears composed of a series of lofty hummocks: three mountains tower above all, evidently extinct volcanoes, exhausted, I hope,

* "Life," i. 199.

now and for ever. From these, spurs wooded and green, descend to the water's edge, and the gullies are rich with vegetation. I saw for the first time lofty palms, one of the chief characteristics of the tropics. We were steering near enough to distinguish with our glasses houses and churches, windmills and *usines* for sugar-works. The French are, I believe, generally better colonisers than ourselves. I was told that no one is permitted to be idle here; an individual, if not engaged, is set to labour on the roads or other public works, until he enters some other service. Poor Josephine the Empress, and her first husband De Beauharnais, were natives of Martinique, and an obelisk was pointed out as having been erected to her memory.

Soon after we approach the island a deep bay opens to view; this is Port Royal or Fort Royal [*] (I find that it is written both ways); at the head of it is the capital of the same name. It is one of the finest harbours, and the only dry dock in the West Indies; so that when our ships require repair, they are sent here. This is not as it should be. Port Royal Bay was the great rendezvous of the French or English fleets as the case might be, for

---

[*] So called from a fort erected there in 1665. See *Naval Chronicle*, ix. 201.

Martinique, like most of the West India Islands, has been alternately in the possession of both countries. Captured by the English in 1762, restored in the following year; in 1794 re-captured, and again restored at the peace of Amiens; once more taken in 1810, and finally restored by the treaty of Paris. You can imagine the size of the bay which could contain the Count de Grasse's fleet, and a fleet of merchantmen besides.

I have obtained a good deal of information from Southey's "Chronological History of the West Indies," which the Captain has lent me; and the perusal of events which have occurred in these parts has greatly increased the interest which I before felt in the West Indies. What a sight to have beheld this mighty armament standing out of such a bay under a cloud of canvas, and the patient British Admiral watching from afar the signals from his frigates that the enemy was under weigh! Four days after, those gallant ships were torn and riddled with shot, and their decks streaming with blood.

"On the morning of the 8th of April, 1782, the signal flew through the chain of frigates stationed between St. Lucia and Martinique, that the enemy's fleet had unmoored, and were proceeding to sea. Upon this, the British fleet, at that moment in complete readiness, took up its anchors, and in little more than two hours was standing towards the enemy with all the sail it could crowd." *

The policy of the French commander was not to engage until the junction of the fleets had been effected. Rodney, however, came up with him on the 9th, and forced on a partial action. Two of the French ships of the line were disabled, and a third was rendered useless by an accident. After this the fleets separated, but the critical character of the occasion called forth all the energy of the British Admiral. It was an absolute necessity to arrest the progress of the enemy. He stood away to the southward during the night, and at daylight on the 12th he had the happiness to find that his evolution had succeeded. He had gained the wind of the enemy, and immediately made the signal to engage. Rodney determined to attempt a manœuvre unprecedented in naval tactics: that of breaking through the enemy's line, which he carried out with complete success, leading into action in his flag-ship. The battle commenced at 7 A.M., and lasted till 6.30 P.M. The British Admiral in the *Formidable* engaged the French Admiral's ship, the *Ville de Paris*, and compelled

* Blane, i. 124.

her to strike.* The result was six ships of the line and two frigates taken, the dispersion of the rest, and the surrender of the Count de Grasse. There were 5,400 troops on board the French fleet.

"The carnage," writes Sir Gilbert Blane, who was by the side of Lord Rodney during the greater part of that eventful day, "on board the prizes is dreadful. By the best accounts, the *Ville de Paris* had nearly three hundred men killed and wounded. The *Glorieux*, when boarded, presented a scene of complete horror. The numbers killed were so great, that the decks were covered with the blood and mangled limbs of the dead, as well as the wounded and dying."

The loss of the British on both days was 261 killed, and 837 wounded; whilst that of the French was estimated at 14,000 taken, killed, or otherwise *hors de combat.*

Now we are abreast of an isolated rock, which

---

* This ship was a present given by the City of Paris to Louis XV. In compliment to the donors, the King named her the *Ville de Paris*. Neither pains nor expense were spared to render the gift worthy of that great city, and of the monarch to whom it was presented. She is stated to have cost £176,000. She carried 106 guns, was larger than any of our first-rates, and copper-bottomed. She had 1,300 men on board at the time of her capture. This magnificent ship and the *Glorieux* foundered in a dreadful gale on the 5th October, 1782, and Admiral Graves's flag-ship, *Ramilies*, was lost at the same time.— Note to Mundy's "Life of Lord Rodney."

might tell some strange tales; it stands a perpetual memorial of British courage and energy. This is the Diamond Rock, probably so called from its shape, and a very rough diamond it is. It stands within three-quarters of a mile of the coast, and is something less than a mile in circumference, and 600 feet high. In 1804, Commodore (afterwards Viscount) Hood, finding that French ships often escaped him, and succeeded in making Port Royal Bay by running in between this rock and the shore, resolved to take possession of it.

A reference to Southey's "History"* will enable us to appreciate the difficulty of the operation. The south, or sea face, is described as hopelessly inaccessible, and the east side as nearly similar; the west side was the only one where a landing could be effected, and even that at considerable danger; the men were obliged to creep through crannies round to the north-west side, at the risk of breaking their necks at every step. On the north-west side there is a slope with a grove of fig-trees; an immense cave overhangs the grove, which the

* iii. 268. An account of the rock by an artist, who, for the purpose of making sketches, resided there for a month by permission of Commodore Hood, Commander-in-Chief of the Station, will be found in *Nav. Chron.* xii. 205, and Captain Morris's "Report of the Loss of the *Diamond*," in ibid. xv. 125.

commander of the rock occupied as his quarters. Notwithstanding these formidable obstacles, a 24-pounder was mounted, commanding the entrance and nearly the whole of the bay. From this battery a covered way was constructed, leading to another with a 24-pounder. The only communication between these batteries was by means of a rope ladder. Another 24-pounder was erected midway up the rock. Thence the ascent to the top winds through shrubs and crags, and on the summit were two long 18-pounders and a flagstaff. The process by which these guns were brought up was ingenious, and such as British seamen only could effect. H.M.S. *Centaur* was brought close under, and a cable was fastened on the top of the rock, which served as a stay for the passage of travellers, to which the gun was lashed, and then heaved up from the *Centaur's* deck by a purchase fastened on the rock. On his Majesty's birthday the British ensign was displayed on the flagstaff, a royal salute was fired, and the rock formally put in commission as a sloop-of-war, with its complement of officers and men.

The water on the rock was not drinkable, so tanks had to be built. Despite these difficulties, and amidst serpents, lizards, bats, and insects innumerable, the rock was held by the gallant crew for one year, and borne on the books of the Admiralty as "His Majesty's Ship *Diamond Rock.*"

The French determined at length to clear the rock of its troublesome occupants. The *Martinico Gazette* of the 14th June, 1805, gives a long account of the investment. It appears that two seventy-fours, a frigate, and a brig, with two hundred soldiers, composed the expedition. The gallant little garrison, under its commandant, Lieutenant Morris—his name ought to be recorded—held out for three days against this overwhelming force, and then was compelled to capitulate for want of ammunition and water. The enemy during the siege had 31 men killed and 40 wounded; the British, 2 killed and 1 wounded.

The waters that wash these shores have been crimsoned with blood, and the annals of the fair lands tell one unbroken tale of man's rapacity. The concluding paragraph in Southey is impressive:—

"The history of the West Indies presents little more than a melancholy series of calamities and crimes. The islands have been laid waste by hurricanes, and visited by pestilence; but the sufferings which have arisen from natural causes are trifling and few in comparison with those which moral and political circumstances have produced. When the horrors of the conquest were over, the Caribs extirpated, and the bucaneers suppressed, these colonies became the seat of war whenever hostilities occurred between the great European powers; and in addition to this evil, a system of slavery took root there, the mitigation and gradual removal of which is one of the most difficult duties that any legislature has ever had to propose."

Before leaving Martinique we got a sight of St. Pierre on the north-west coast, as I am informed a very handsome town, with a population larger than that of Port Royal.

CHAPTER VI.

ST. THOMAS'S.—JACMEL.

Tuesday, June 2nd.—A pretty strong breeze arose last evening, but I kept my port open all night, nevertheless. We must have passed close to several islands, Dominica, Guadaloupe, Montserrat, and others; but as I saw nothing of them, I shall say nothing about them.

Rain falls heavily all this morning, and the decks are so wet that we are forced to remain below, and I fancy that those experienced in tropical weather are careful of getting wet. The gangway by the fore-hatch is always a resource and a resort under these circumstances; but the sky cleared at mid-day, and at 4 P.M. St. Thomas's was right ahead of us. A ridge of detached rocks, extending in front of the island, has, at a distance, the appearance of a breakwater. After passing it, we noticed a boat upset and four men clinging to the keel. Our engines were instantly stopped, and the mail-boat ordered to be cleared away; but at that moment the occupants of a little pleasure schooner caught sight of the accident, and, having the wind, bore swiftly down and picked up the men. As sharks abound here, their position was one, perhaps, not altogether desirable.

We hang out our ensign, and hoist the distinguishing pendant, enter the harbour, and anchor in the middle. This is a busy port; several steamers were lying there, and the bunting of many nations was floating on the masts of the merchantmen. The harbour is land-locked, being nearly surrounded by lofty hills rising precipitately, which give it almost the appearance of a lake. The town—not very large, with a population of about 16,000—is crowded along the water's edge with houses of all shapes and sizes, and straggles up three hills at its back. Here and there are some more pretentious mansions standing in the midst of gardens. It has a lively appearance; bright colours predominate. The houses are painted white, the jalousies green, and the shingles* of the roofs are dyed red, for the sake of preserving them. The island ori-

* Slips of pine-wood, imported generally from North America, used almost universally for roofing throughout the West Indies.

ginally belonged to the Dutch; the town bears a strong resemblance to a Dutch toy, and its temperature to a Dutch oven.

St. Thomas's is one of the group discovered by Columbus in his second voyage, in 1493, on which he bestowed the name of The Virgin Islands, in allusion to the legend in the Romish ritual. It was successively possessed by Dutch and English bucaneers, but they quitted it, and it was ultimately settled by the Danes in 1672. They possess, also, the adjoining islands of St John's and Santa Cruz, their sole possessions in the West Indies; the latter having been purchased of the French for £75,000. The Danish islands were taken by the British in 1801, and again in 1807, and were not restored till 1815. Considering the important station which St. Thomas's now occupies, one is tempted to regret that it was not retained. In 1867 the Government of the United States entered into a negotiation to purchase the island. Denmark was willing to *sell*, and so were the United States. When the amount of dollars had been agreed upon, greenbacks were found deficient, and "one more repudiation of agreement was noted in Jonathan's account-book," as I read somewhere. The Danish Government is apparently regardless of æsthetics, and little seems to be done beyond receiving the revenue, which must be considerable. A taste for flagstaffs prevails extensively, every store seemed to possess one.

Our starboard side facing the town was invested, or rather infested, by shore-boats. Off came the woolly-haired boatmen by scores, in white shirts and trousers, jabbering and pushing in the stems of their boats as though the fate of empires depended on their exertions. Bumboats with vegetables and fruit, lettuces, bananas, and oranges, come alongside; some of these had negresses sitting in the stern-sheets, to superintend the disposal of their wares; for the most part stately-looking dames wearing broad straw hats, or bandana handkerchiefs of bright colours, arranged somewhat as the French *poissardes* wear them.

We hurried over our dinner, and some of us jumped into a boat, not without a desperate contest as to which one should have the honour of conveying us. Provided with our white umbrellas, for the sun was still exceedingly powerful, we were rowed to the jetty, and I trod for the first time on West Indian ground. We repaired at once to the Moravian book-store. The early-closing system prevails here, and the librarian, a minister of that denomination, whom we found seated at tea with his wife, told us that the store closed at five, but he was willing to reopen the shutters for us. We found a good assortment of books. Tauchnitz editions abounded, of which we made several purchases.

The streets reminded me of those of a French provincial town, except in cleanliness, and there these had the advantage, though not quite so sweet as they might be, notwithstanding that the Danish police regulations are said to be very stringent. Some of the principal houses were pretty, surrounded by gardens, and with verandahs covered with creepers. A love of horticulture as well as of flagstaffs is everywhere displayed. The shops, or rather stores, which is the proper designation out here, with the names of many nationalities superscribed, were generally closed. The negro population looks thriving: tall well-made people, the women especially, who from their habit—a characteristic of their race—of carrying burdens on their heads, hold themselves remarkably upright. They are not handsome; flattened noses and protuberant lips indelibly mark their origin; they are all singularly alike in appearance. A fondness for dress is very noticeable in both sexes; the men delight in European costume, so ill adapted to this climate. A tall hat, a black tight-fitting dress-coat, and as tight Wellington boots with high heels, are the *acmé* of nigger gentility. Their linen always seems very white; it may be from the contrast with their skin.

> " So shall their brighter hues contrast the glow
> Of the dusk bosoms that beat high below."
> BYRON, *The Island*.

The ladies are much addicted to gaudy colours, jewellery, and long skirts. You may see a tall black woman with a train sweeping the ground; she probably wears neither shoes nor stockings, but she strides along—the only scavenger I saw, for she considers it beneath her dignity to raise her dress above the mud and filth. An English lady who did so was pointed at as "a mean thing."

After a stroll along the main street and peering into some of its arteries, we enter the principal hostelry, Hôtel du Commerce, to get "a drink," for out here one acquires the American habit of "liquoring up." Whilst waiting to be served, I noticed a remarkably fine dog; he stood as high as the tables; in shape he resembled a bloodhound. I spoke of his handsome appearance to the owner, and asked, "Is he a Cuban?" "No," he replied, "a Dutch bull-dog." As the animal seemed good-tempered, I patted him and remarked that he was very fat. "Yes," said the gentleman, "in the winter he gets fat, but when the summer comes he loses his flesh." Bless me, I thought, as I stood perspiring at every pore, if this is the cold weather, what must the summer be?

We saw placarded everywhere "ARRIVAL OF THE ELFIN STAR." We made inquiries of the black waiter, and we learnt that this luminary was one of a Company of Players just arrived from the United States, and the first performance was to take place that very night at 7.30. We resolved to attend. The theatre was in Cocoa-nut Square. The *salle* was a somewhat ostentatious building, with a blazing gas star in front. The doors were not yet open, and as there was a considerable assemblage waiting for admission, we thought there might be a rush; so one of our party who had happened to meet the *troupe* in another island, and had made personal acquaintance with its members, introduced himself through the stage-door, saw the manager, and procured tickets for us.

We entered and took our seats, chairs just in front of the orchestra. The tinkling of a bell aroused the musicians into activity. One tall thin young black—a *jeune élégant*—in evening dress and faultless tie, and who sat in the orchestra fanning himself, played the harmonium, not badly, and with much grace of manipulation. Three men, French or Americans I should guess, performed with six hands on one piano; they could not well have managed this, had not the bodkin been a thin lath of a man. Two violins, a flute, and a violoncello completed the instruments, the performers on which found a difficulty in following throughout, and so joined in occasionally—*ad libitum*—whenever they were able.

Half-past eight before the curtain rose; house crammed; audience in high expectation; heat tremendous. All the quality of the place there, but with the exception of two young ladies, who we were informed were English, beauty did not predominate. The gods had been very patient, but negro nature could bear it no longer, and at last pent-up feelings exploded in a regular stamping, just what we call "Kentish fire." I append the play-bill for your edification :—

APOLLO THEATRE!

Manager and Proprietor, W. M. Holland; Business Manager, Harry Morse; Pianist, James O'Neill; Scenic Artist, Hite Walden.

For a short Season only. Return of the Elfin Star, MISS EFFIE JOHNS, and W. M. Holland's Dramatic Co. Opening Night TUESDAY, June 2nd, 1874, on which occasion will be presented for the first time here, Alex. Dumas, Jun.'s great Play of CAMILLE (La Dame au Camélia). Miss Effie Johns as Camille Gautier.

TUESDAY, June 2nd, 1874, CAMILLE, or the Fate of a Coquette.

Camille Gautier, Miss Effie Johns; Armand Duval, Mr. W. M. Holland; Mons. Duval (his Father), Mr. A. A. Armstrong; Count de Varville, Mr. Harry Morse; Gaston, Mr. C. W. Holmes; Gustave, Mr. Hite Walden; Messenger, Mr. J. Jones; Mad Prudence, Miss Lizzie Hardy; Nichette, Mrs. C. W. Holmes; Nanine, Miss Fannie Francis; Olympie, Mrs. C. W. Holmes.

Act 1st—March—The Supper. Act 2nd—April—The Pledge of Love. Act 3rd—August—The Sacrifice. Act 4th—October—The Fête. Act 5th—Winter—The Eleventh Hour.

Prices of Admission:—Boxes containing Six Chairs, $7 50 c.; Parquette Chairs, $1; Gallery, 50 c. Reserved Seats may be secured at the Theatre, daily, from 8 A.M. to 10 A.M., and from 12 N. to 4 P.M.

The Elfin appeared in a luxuriant *chevelure* of light auburn hair, which descended to her waist; such as would have made the fortune of " Mrs. S. A. Allen's World Hair Restorer." I was disappointed to learn from Mr. M—— that it was not a growing crop, but such as may be described as " the light fantastic tow." The acting was very indifferent, yet hardly bad enough to become a burlesque; but I was more amused by watching the countenances of the audience than by the players. The ladies in the stalls were nicely but simply dressed, mostly in white muslin. A little coloured girl just before me had her woolly back-hair contorted into two little tufts, which were bound with bright blue ribbon. The occupants of the gallery behaved very well, for delays between the acts were great; the plot was, I should suppose, utterly unfathomable by them; and the characters such as they could not comprehend. A sentimental five-act French drama was quite out of place here; two screaming farces with plenty of stage-business would have been more appropriate; but the interest evinced by the negroes nevertheless was extraordinary. Alice in Wonderland could scarcely have been more entranced. It was a sight to see the outstretched necks and the protruding eyeballs. A profound silence was generally maintained, but there was great shouting and volleys of "yah! yahs!" and manifestations of white teeth when the lovers had to embrace; this was considered an excellent joke.

There was a well-supplied bar in the lobby, to which all the males resorted between the acts. We sat out "The Supper," "The Pledge of Love," and "The Sacrifice," and deeming that sufficient, we withdrew.

We returned to the hotel, and applied for refreshments; the bar was closed; we were referred to the club, but could gain no admittance there; so we took boat and returned to the steamer. There the lights were extinguished, and the stewards gone to bed, so we had to do the same. The Licensing Bill is now being debated in England: let us hope the legislature will deal gently with hungry and thirsty travellers.

June 3rd.—Continued noise since daybreak; the steam-winch in full occupation all the time. I heard a cry and a rush—something had happened. I jumped out of my berth and looked out of the door. I was informed that the boatswain's mate had had his hand jammed in the chain, and that two of his fingers were torn off. The surgeon was hurrying up the fore-hatchway, and I was preparing to follow, but I was told it was not so bad as reported, but although the poor fellow's hand was much lacerated, he had not lost his fingers.

A courtly negro came on board this morning to dispose of his wares. An imposing-looking man, I should say, in both senses—tall and well dressed in the tight black dress-coat and the Wellington boots, white trousers, and a jaunty Paramatta hat. He had evidently a good opinion of himself—the characteristic of black people—was perfectly civil and well-mannered. His goods consisted of light coats and hats, Habana cigars, slow-match, baskets, fans, shells, bracelets of mimosa seeds and beetles' wings, and those small scarlet seeds with black tips which are so common on Brighton boxes of shells. I never knew before what they were. I was told they were the seeds of the wild liquorice. He had no reason to regret his visit: light coats and fans were in special request. I thought his charges high, and there was a deal of bargaining before a sale was concluded.

It was noon before we got under weigh, and I was glad to get away from the heated atmosphere of this confined harbour.

What an excitement there is in England to-day! I wonder what has won the Derby?

Away again at sea. Rain comes down, there is nothing to see and nothing to do. I went to my cabin and lay on the sofa to read, and of course fell asleep, and so soundly that I missed the dinner-bells. Aroused by the steward, we are only four at the Captain's table, but we manage to entertain ourselves with plenty of conversation. In the evening I am told we are passing Porto Rico.

June 5th.—Awakened at 5 by the firing of one of our signal guns. We were just entering Jacmel Bay, so I hurried up on deck. The Captain sent to ask if I would like to go on shore, an offer which I gladly accepted. Jacmel is a port of Hayti, and that is the western portion of San Domingo or Hispaniola, next to

F

Cuba the largest of all the West Indian Islands. The other portion is the Republic of San Domingo. The island is thus divided into two distinct states, the Eastern or former Spanish portion bearing the title of the Dominican Republic, of which the town of San Domingo is the capital; and the Western—formerly belonging to France—constituting the Republic of Hayti, with Port-au-Prince as its capital. Hayti has been repeatedly the scene of most frightful anarchy and bloodshed, and still is continually distracted by contending parties, the result of independence combined with incapacity for self-government.

A passenger who had traversed the country tells me that in the interior, between ranges of mountains, lie extensive and beautiful plains, intersected by rivers, many of them navigable. The natural products of the island are unlimited in value, the greater part being covered with forests of mahogany, cedar, logwood, and other valuable trees. Mines of hidden wealth in minerals, but none of these are now worked, and Hayti, instead of being, as it once was and might still be, one of the most commercial islands, is reduced to a state of impoverishment and stagnation.

The mail-boat, with the British ensign at her stern, led the way; I followed in another of the ship's boats with two Haytian gentlemen. "*Pauvre Jacmel!*" sighed out audibly one of them, who had been for some years away at Paris, as we neared the town. The bay is surrounded on three sides by hills covered with stunted trees or scrub; about the centre, amidst a sprinkling of cocoa-nut palms, is the town—containing a population of about 13,000, as one of the Haytians told me—the rickety-looking wooden jetty of which we were now approaching. Two short but stout soldiers lolling on their arms guarded the exit, but took no notice of us. Their uniform consisted of double-breasted buttoned-up blue tunics with stiff collars, coarse blue cloth trousers, and shakos with a ball and shaving-brush plume, no shoes or stockings, which I thought the only sensible part of their costume, if I may so express myself.

I took leave of my Haytian fellow-passengers, and followed where the officers in charge of the mails had preceded.

Such streets—their ways certainly require mending—they were paved to be sure, but like the bed of a water-course after the torrent has passed. Much rain had evidently fallen, mud was everywhere, filth abounded. I went hopping about from point to point, slipping here upon a slimy bit of stone, then sousing into slush over my ankles. Although *pumps* might be useful, defend me from thin shoes here, and I incautiously had come in my white deck ones. I stopped to wonder at a herd of swine, I mean a sow and her numerous family. You know the sort of pig we admire at home—short legs and a compact body with a little curly tail, small eyes twinkling amidst furbelows of fat, and then the shortest of snouts—but these presented a strange contrast to the *beau idéal*. I suppose this was not a remarkable breed, but that all Haytian pigs are the same. The mother was about the height of a young donkey, her children long-legged in proportion, in colour white spotted with black. I wish I had the pencil of an artist to draw them. Their long attenuated snouts—like those of ant-eaters—were admirably adapted for poking into the holes and crevices of the roads, which they were doing as I came by. Perhaps here, too, pigs are the only scavengers of the Republic—as vultures are elsewhere—but then they ought to be prosecuted for not doing their duty, though I don't believe Jacmel has a Board of Works or even a Vestry to take cognisance of the matter. Now the sow looked up to me with large vacant eyes, hungry perhaps, poor thing. Street garbage may not be a nutritious diet, and she was as thin as a greyhound, and like one in shape; her middle was really as if two sides of bacon were stuck together, and nothing between them; then, as a compensating balance to the long snout, there was a lengthy downright straight tail. Now if you can picture to yourself such a creature as this, and ten or twelve juvenile porkers, the diminutive counterparts of their—I dare say—amiable parent, you will not be surprised that I, as a traveller anxious for information, should have stopped in the mud to observe and remark upon the animal productions of the country. If a pig-show should ever be contemplated at the Crystal Palace, the attendance of a Haytian sow and party should certainly be secured.

A long story this, you will say, about a pig; but I was so much amused, that I lost sight of H.M.'s Mails altogether. I slid about through devious streets in all directions, the same in aspect, and all equally dirty. Jacmel resembles a Spanish town—white or whity-brown two-storied stuccoed houses with verandahs and jalousies, and shops or stores in arches. The day is still early, and few persons are about. Here comes a brown girl driving a donkey with panniers of vegetables, wretched-looking animals both of them. My Haytian acquaintances, in reply to my inquiry in the boat as to a white wall on the top of the hill above the town, replied with some ostentation, "*C'est l'Arsenal;*" but I had no fancy to scale the hill to see it. There, I suppose, those two soldiers are quartered, and when they are away the garrison is denuded, so that I might inspect the troops as well on the jetty as by climbing the hill. A long-legged man passes me riding a small lean pony. I observed that there were holsters with pistols at the saddle-bow; this is significant of the pleasant condition of things in the country. The pony in substance and mould is similar to the pig breed, that is, of the greyhound shape. Balance and the crupper alone preserve the equilibrium of the saddle, I presume; for the girths were quite loose.

By dint of inquiries in French and English I at last found the post-office, where the officers were seated and busy with the post-master. I waited till they came out, and we returned to the pier. Just as we were pushing off an English consular agent, who had just ridden in from the country, hailed the officers and said, "You must not land any goods on your return, as you will be in quarantine, owing to small-pox in Jamaica!" Pleasant news! A poor blackey wanted to come off as a passenger with us, but an official sternly interdicted his departure, as he had not a passport, nor I presume *de quoi* to bribe the officer. He looked so wistfully at us—we hung back a bit—but the official was inexorable, and he had the army to support him— for the two soldiers were still on duty there, so that we had to leave him behind continuing to urge his suit. Here is a land of liberty!

I believe we are distant from Jamaica only something over two hundred miles. The Captain says we shall see the light off Morant Point at about 1 o'clock in the morning. I begin to pack; generally there is something odious in the idea of packing; but now it is quite exhilarating, for I must own it, I have had more than enough of sea life, and long to be on shore again.

Happening to be awake at 1 A.M., I looked out of the port, and sure enough there was the light, and so I may exclaim with Canon Kingsley, "At last!"

CHAPTER VII.

JAMAICA.

Saturday, June 6th.—I had bathed before six, and then was engrossed in collecting odds and ends in my cabin, and ramming them into nooks of my baggage. Sea air seems to have swelled my clothes, or I am not so skilful a packer as useful hands at home, and I have to adopt the ultimate resource of standing in my portmanteau. So it was that I had allowed Port Royal to be passed unobserved, although I was sensible of the engines having been stopped for awhile. I now looked out of the port, and saw Kingston just ahead of us. A knock at my door, my name is mentioned hypothetically, "Come in," and there stood B——before me. He had been on duty at Port Royal, had hailed the steamer from a boat, and boarded her. How warmly we met! Although his head was protected by a pith helmet, his face was radiant with heat. We had much information to exchange, and then we ascended to the upper deck. We were stopped on our way by the especial invitation of some of my young friends among the ship's officers, to partake of a farewell "cocktail" in their cabin. It was early for potation, but such hospitality could not be declined. They had been most kind and attentive to me. The materials were at hand, and with a swizzle-stick an effervescing draught was quickly prepared, and as quickly dispatched, with many expressed wishes for health and prosperity.

And now on deck: what a scene! I was charmed with all I saw. First of all I will try and give you some idea of the approach to Kingston. It stands in the north centre of a land-locked bay, about six miles long, and two wide; almost a lagune, formed on the seaside by a narrow spit of land not much more than a sand-bank, called The Palisades, running east and west from the coast-line. At its western extremity it widens out. At the point of this spit is Port Royal, and after rounding this is the not very wide entrance to Port Royal Bay, or Kingston Harbour. Vessels coming from the eastward, as ours was, have therefore to double this spit in order to get up to Kingston. The depth of water in the bay is so great, that a huge steamer, like the *Nile*, drawing twenty-one feet, could range close alongside of the wharf.

The aspect of the island is beautiful—almost everything looks beautiful under a powerful sunlight. I cannot say, however, that Kingston contributes much to the beauty of the scene. Its straight parallel streets, teeming with life, run down at right angles to the water's edge. There is nothing striking or picturesque about it; it extends along the flat, but the sure signs of the tropics are here—lofty palm-trees dotted about in all directions. On looking upwards there are such hills, or rather mountains, clothed to their summits in luxuriant verdure, white houses here and there peeping out from their green sides, and lights and shadows so diversified on ridges and ravines; they seem to slope up gradually from the town. B—— points out to me, far away on the heights, the hut barracks of Newcastle (whither we were bound) like white stones shining out in the darkness, or a flock of distant sheep in the Highlands, and upwards still, the "Blue Mountains," with clouds reposing on their summits.

It was hot, blistering. The confusion around was distracting. The woolly heads of a host of negro boys and men were popping up and down in the water, like corks thrown overboard, and I envied the position; their owners with extended arms were vociferating to us on deck to throw silver into the water (they didn't say copper, like our mudlarks) for them to dive after, and it was surprising how quickly they reappeared with the coin. The abused but invaluable steam-winch was incessant in its noise and duties in discharging cargo. A broad landing-stage from the steamer to the quay made entrance easy, and many elegant blacks and whites came to solicit our patronage. That most inevitable and obnoxious process of coaling had commenced as soon as we were alongside; a continuous stream of black men and women, chiefly young, for the labour is excessive, were hurrying up and down with coal-baskets on their heads, chattering, laughing, and showing their teeth all the while, with features the same as I have before described, *ex uno disce omnes*, but well-limbed, muscular people, and above our average height. A check-taker is stationed at the foot of the landing-stage, and, as they pass, each coal-bearer calls out his or her number before emptying their baskets into a slide in the side of the ship. The noise and dust of this operation are something portentous. These coaling men and women are, I believe, the lowest of the population. They work at this process day and night without ceasing until it is completed; their pay is high, as it ought to be, something over five shillings a day, I think, and when it is over they spend their wages in dissipation, and do nothing else until the next vessel arrives.

B—— and I were so hungry that we were delighted when at last the bell rang at 9 o'clock for breakfast, and we did ample justice to the abundant fare spread before us. B—— had brought a pine-apple as a present for the Captain, but as there was another there already for him, we demolished this one, for the Captain was too busy to join us. Then we arose. I wished all my associates that I could find good-bye. I left all my warm clothing and rugs with the steward until my return, and we stepped on shore.

B—— had hired a buggy, a vehicle so called here, and a carriage greatly in vogue—a light thing on high wheels, and a head after the American model. My luggage was placed on the seat in front, the black driver whisked his pair of light, active horses, and away we went through the streets, as dingy, dirty, gloomy ones as I ever encountered. There seems to be a want of energy here. Perhaps the climate has much to do with it, but imagine a large rich town in the British dominions, with British inhabitants, without gas, when that little Danish town of St. Thomas's is in full enjoyment of it. And as I observed before, there is no twilight in these latitudes: when the sun sets it is dark, so that there is special need of illumination.

We drove first to Macdonald's, the great saddler of the place, and then to the provision warehouse of Messrs. Alberga, most obliging people. The hospitality of the West Indies is proverbial; here was my first proof of it:—We exclaimed about the heat, with some allusion to the thirst it occasioned. Immediately a cooling drink was ordered and prepared, of which our acceptance was requested. In a few minutes it was brought in tumblers, and offered to us—Moselle and seltzer, flavoured with slices of pine-apple, and lumps of ice. It was indeed acceptable and most refreshing.

Then off again in the buggy, passing ugly buildings, an ugly church, ugly everything; but now we are in the suburbs, the green hills are before us, and the sides of the road are studded with detached villas, some of them very pretty, painted white or yellow, with green verandahs, standing in gardens, shaded with graceful trees, and rich with every colour of plant and creeper, and for fences there are rows of pinguins (so

B—— tells me they are called, and that their botanical name is *bromelia*), with long sharp-spiked leaves, like those amidst which pine-apples grow. With such a protection it is unnecessary to hang out a notice that "Trespassers will be prosecuted"—*noli me tangere* with a vengeance. Some gardens, again, are hedged in with rows of cactus, not like those you see in England growing in flower-pots, but great thumping stalks, fifteen feet high, set close together—an impracticable bullfinch for the most impetuous of horsemen. The roads are full of people passing to and fro. The majority, I should say, were women, and most of these have baskets on their heads. They have a peculiar jaunty gait, perhaps from carrying weights. You have observed, I dare say, the walk of the London milk-women under the oppression of the cans suspended from the yoke: it is like that, only the negresses are much more graceful. They are generally well dressed, and when proceeding on their work, tie a handkerchief round their hips, and draw their skirts through it, thus forming a furbelow round their waists not unbecoming. Their legs are thus bared from the knee downwards, and they step out in a style which would gladden the heart of the most exacting drill-sergeant. They appear so contented and good-tempered, their eyes are always turned towards the passer-by, as they greet you with a smile and a "Marnin', sar!" There are also a great many light carts on the road, drawn by one or two horses or mules; sometimes one in the shafts, and a smaller one as an outrigger, to help or impede, as the case might be; the drivers sitting under the shade of large umbrella straw hats.

The roads were macadamised and in good order, and we bowled along at a rattling rate. We pulled up at a house where some friends of B—— live. Mounting the steps, we entered the verandah of a very pretty house in a shady nook. I fancy the houses of the gentry out here are all pretty nearly on the same plan: a habitable verandah all round, and the drawing and dining rooms in the centre, and green jalousies at the windows, which are unglazed. Having paid our respects, we sped on our way. A two-hours' drive from Kingston brought us to a halting-place called "The Gardens," a convenient half-way house to Newcastle. Here are Bolton's stables, and I may say that even here we met with a *cordial* reception, for we were offered a glass of gin! Our little horses live here when they are at home; and that, as in the case of the Pickwickian cab-horse, "is not werry often," I should think, judging by their ribs and legs. Here we take leave of wheels, for the remainder of the distance can be performed only by walking or riding. Here also is a bar where thirsty souls can be refreshed, and where crackers (light, dry biscuits) can be had for the asking, provided you run up an account.

The halt could not be devoid of interest to me, it was so novel a life. Under the lee of Bolton's somewhat uncouth range of stabling, I sat and watched the loading of my luggage on a couple of mules; black hostlers were rubbing down horses; luggage mules were straying about, ill-used-looking creatures—negroes are said to be cruel not only to animals, but to their children; laden men and women were passing up and down; but nature was in full luxuriance here: so rich a prospect my eyes had never feasted on before. We are in a valley surrounded by hills—the Liguanean Mountains. I look down the gorge on my left; it is dense with intricate verdure; cotton-trees, palms, and broad-leafed bananas stand prominent. I look up the valley and to the hills, and there is water bursting out from the top, and leaping down from rock to rock, gleaming in the sunlight, until lost in the close vegetation.

Our nags were now brought out. I mounted B——'s clever little blood-horse "Nimble," and he one of Bolton's, which was to be mine during my stay—called by the apparently inappropriate name of "Beethoven." We had each a "waterproof" strapped to the saddle-bow. No one moves without one here. There is danger in getting wet, which produces fever and ague, and in this hilly climate heavy storms of rain come on so suddenly. We passed the post-office and the "Piquet House" at Gordon Town, a halting-place for troops on the march; here was a guard of the 2nd West India Regiment—fine, big men. Now and then we were able to canter for a few hundred yards, but except that, it was one continuous climb. The air feels purer and cooler as we ascend. "The Gardens" are 900 feet above the level: the point to which we have to attain is 4,130. The road winds round the hills, cut out on the face of the limestone. I look upon fearful precipices, down which one false step of the horse might hurl me. We pass several teams of mules, the drivers always civil and smiling. The road, or, more correctly, the path, is, as we advanced, wide enough for only two horses to pass, and not always that. We pass through the hamlet of Middleton, where the Duke of Buckingham has property; where

G

there is a *barbecue*, as it is termed, being a broad terrace or platform, on which coffee-berries are exposed to the heat of the sun. Four times we crossed the little river Hope, which flows through the mountains. The scenery is quite charming. Sometimes the road winds round masses of rocks; at others it is skirted and fringed with clumps of mangoes, orange-trees, bananas, and frangipani, and trees, plants, and flowers with so many hard names are pointed out, that they escape my recollection. Perhaps B—— might have been inventing them for his own amusement; at all events, I should not detect them, for I am sorry to say that I am not strong in botany. One great beauty here is the variety of creepers, which hang so gracefully from bough to bough, and unite the whole mass in delicate tracery. It is in truth a garden of Eden run wild.

An hour and a half's ride brought us to Newcastle. This is merely a military station on the heights, its locality having been selected for sanitary reasons. It is composed of rows of white huts one above the other. First we come upon the Artillery quarters, then those of the Infantry. The head-quarters of the 97th, and a portion of the 98th, are stationed here. Leaving them, we wind round a path so steep that I twist my fingers into the animal's mane to make progress easier; we turn a sharp angle, enter a little garden, ride round to the front of a hut, and there is a loving soul standing on the threshold to greet us with all the fervour of woman's affection.

CHAPTER VIII.

NEWCASTLE.

Sunday, June 7th.—You may easily believe that I slept soundly last night. I was awoke by the barking of the dogs, caused by their master's voice. B—— put his head in at my open window, and asked if I would like to get up and bathe. "By all means." So jumping out of bed, and flinging on a few clothes, I quickly joined him.

My first inaugural morning at Newcastle, and such a one! A bright speckless sky and a blazing sun. The bath-house was about a thousand yards ahead of us: we can see it perched on the opposite hill as we pass through the wicket of the little garden.

I shall weary you with my descriptions, and after all they are but very faint representations of what I see and what I wish to convey. Well, no matter. On my left is a hill which rises abruptly; it is covered with trees, not of any great size; a rill of water is trickling down from it, collected into pipes to supply the station. On our right we look down a spacious valley, little white habitations appearing here and there amidst the green, bounded, as far as the eye can reach, by purple mountains. Before us rises Catherine's Peak; to its base we are wending our way, and through what a garden we are proceeding! The whole surrounding has, to me, quite an exotic appearance, with a greenhouse feel and temperature; and the fresh flush of vegetable fragrance, with the pure atmosphere, promotes a buoyant and elastic state of mind and body, with a consequent exhilaration of spirit. Bright wide-coned daturas and bushes of lively-coloured begonias; the hibiscus, with its gorgeous scarlet flowers, ferns and fern-trees, creepers innumerable, chiefly convolvuli, springing in spontaneous luxuriance. There are scarlet geraniums, but I am told they are not indigenous, but were imported by an officer formerly quartered here. What one would not expect to find here, are the common white clover and modest violet, and gorse which grows above the height of my head. We stopped short in a charming little nook to listen to the piping of a humming-bird, perched upon the leafless branch of a tree; the sweet little warbler was whistling his morning song, and turning round his head as if in order to be heard in all directions. Then a great emperor butterfly sailing by seemed to discompose him, and away he flew.

A slight rise on the adjacent hill brought us to the bath, constructed by the liberality of the agent of Dr. Hamilton, on whose estate it is situated, for the use of the officers. It is enclosed by high rails: at one end a shed and bench for the convenience of dressing. The bath is about forty feet long, and deep enough at one end to plunge in. A constant stream of water flows in from the hill. The atmosphere being so hot, the water strikes one as being very cold; it was, however, extremely refreshing. Then we hurried back to dress and breakfast, to be ready for Divine Service, which is performed in the school-room of the Infantry barracks at 9.15. The chaplain has to ride from his residence on another hill, across the valley through which we rode yesterday; it is an hour's journey, and he has to return for the service at Craigton Church: hence the early hour of our service. The officers and the ladies and children sit in front, the men behind. The service was short, but most reverently performed, closed by a brief and excellent sermon. I observed, by-the-bye, that the clergyman introduced into the Litany "earthquakes," after "lightning and tempest." The music of the hymns was supplied by a portion of the band of the 97th, and so admirably in unison, that not having looked back, I thought it proceeded from an harmonium skilfully played. The congregation joined generally in the singing, for the tunes were such as are well known. "Rock of Ages" was one of them, which I never hear without remembering Mr. Gladstone's exquisite version, framed, I believe, after the model of the rhymed Latin hymns of the early Church:—

> "Nil in manu mecum fero,
> Sed me versus crucem gero;
> Vestimenta nudus oro,
> Opem debilis imploro;
> Fontem Christi quæro immundus,
> Nisi laves, moribundus.
> Dum hos artus vita regit;
> Quando nox sepulchro tegit;
> Mortuos cum stare jubes,
> Sedens Judex inter nubes;
> Jesus, pro me perforatus,
> Condar intra tuum latus."

I beg your pardon for introducing Latin, as I know it is not your *forte*, but my pen ran away. Perhaps you will say it required mending. Well, I won't do it again.

In the afternoon we had several visitors, and

we sat out in the little garden and had tea. What an exquisite prospect lay before us! From this elevated position we look down over an amphitheatre of hills, and we can trace the deep windings of the valley at their base, down to the sea; we look over Kingston, and the bay, the Palisades, Port Royal, and a long range of sea-coast to the west; and we can trace the high-road from Kingston to Spanish Town. I think I have read somewhere that when Columbus wished to give Isabella of Spain a description of the appearance of Jamaica, he is reported to have crumpled up a piece of paper, and to have placed it before the Queen as a correct delineation of the island, as I should say it was. Bee humming-birds flit from flower to flower, just like "the busy bee;" their bodies are not larger than a *bumble*, and they hum just like it. Every now and then a sluggish buzzard, John Crows as they are called here, comes floating by. These birds are ugly, but useful in consuming carrion and other impurities. They are, therefore, protected by law; a fine of £3 is attached to the wanton destruction of them. In consequence of their immunity they fly almost within arm's reach of us; a peculiarity which strikes me about these birds is, that they never seem to flap their wings. While engrossed with all I saw and heard around me, mosquitoes took the opportunity of welcoming the stranger, and my feet and hands were objects of their particular attention.

The evenings are delicious here, and the canopy above brilliant with stars. Turning towards the sea, the Southern Cross is on my left hand, and the Wain upon the right. As soon as the sun sinks behind the hills darkness overshadows the face of the land, except when the moon is on duty, and then her pale light throws the outlines of the hills into relief, and far away she flashes on the water, making the bay resplendent, as though it were polished steel, and the eye detects, as our laureate sings—

" Silver sails all out of the West,
Under the silver moon."

"Deep night, dark night, the silent of the night"—no, not "silent:" I am quoting Shakspere now, but the last epithet does not apply, for as the sun disappears, then forthwith uprises a concert —the performers awaiting, as it were, the great conductor's signal to commence—in the bush, in the garden, in the grass, in the scrub all round; myriads of crickets, grasshoppers, and I suppose other green things, chirp and croak incessantly, and who "won't go home till morning, till daylight doth appear." I should have thought that all the hoarse-voiced frogs of the Pontine Marshes "assisted," only my friends say they never saw any frogs in this locality, but the noise—come from whatever it may—is incessant, ubiquitous.* Fireflies—a species of the glowworm of our summer evenings, I presume—abound in this region; they flit and sparkle in all directions, like myriads of restless elfin torch-bearers. So I have a concert and an illumination, this latter very beautiful to behold, every night without the asking:—

> " And every hedge and copse is bright,
> With the quick firefly's playful light;
> Like thousands of the sparkling gems
> Which blaze in Eastern diadems."

They enter my bedroom sometimes, and in the dark they fly so near the mosquito curtains, that one would fancy that they would set them on fire, but they are perfectly innocuous. The body, about the size of a wasp's, is of a greyish colour. I caught one once, and examined it, and it appeared to me that the luminous matter is emitted from beneath the wings. I have heard

---

* Possibly the chief vocalist may be 'the " Gecko, or croaking lizard, a nocturnal animal," which I have since seen mentioned in Gosse's " Naturalist in Jamaica," p. 75.

that the negroes collect them in a covered wine-glass or tumbler, and make use of them in lieu of candles. I also heard of a lady who placed them in little muslin bags, and with them ornamented her hair and dress, and in this brilliant *toilette* she appeared at a ball. Report says the little animals were let loose afterwards, none the worse for the service they had rendered.

I am thoroughly enjoying myself here; the pure air and the healthy mode of life make me capable of appreciating everything. The early bath is quite a pleasant reunion—a water-party, in fact—and we have much fun and chat between the plunges. Then there is generally a long walk with some object to see, which deprives it of the "constitutional" character which I dislike, and a ride in the afternoon. There is a croquet ground close by, constructed, I believe, by an officer of the Royal Engineers, and there several of us assembled one afternoon to be photographed by a gunner of the Artillery.

As we pass onwards, leaving the bath-house on the right, there are traces of encampment, where troops were put under canvas when fever was rife. The circles made by the tents are still discernible. Not far from this there is a little plot of ground, cleared from the surrounding bush, enclosed by stout palings, and kept neat. This contains the turfed graves of those who succumbed to "the pestilence that walketh in darkness," and to "the sickness that destroyeth in the noonday." Then beyond are the lovely "fern walks," so called, where in umbrageous solitudes acres and acres are covered with dense vegetation. Here are fern-trees in their greatest beauty; they grow only, I believe, in these elevated regions, and they look much better when massed with other trees than when alone; for their stems are mere bare poles. Here the enthusiast in ferns will be gratified by the great variety of fronds. What strikes one as remarkable in these woods is the absence of animal life; not a rat nor a winged fowl, nor a wild goat, nor a coney, for which the "high hills" and "stony rocks" are said to be a refuge, crosses your path, where in such thickets one would expect that a startled deer or a tusked boar would be aroused from its lair; that ring-tailed monkeys would be swinging from tree to tree, or the chattering of gaily-plumed parrots be heard. These things were once here, no doubt, but they are now extinct,* and, as far

* Not the parrots, for Gosse writes: "Flocks of green parrots and parroquets, among the pimento-trees," p. 65.

as the quiet enjoyment of these "walks" is concerned, it is perhaps as well that the tusked boar or other wild beasts glaring at you and preparing to make their fatal spring, or venomous reptiles, should not be found there.

Tuesdays are band-days here, that is, the band of the 97th plays at 3 o'clock in front of the mess-house, when all comers are welcomed by the officers. Many ladies and gentlemen ride in from distant points to attend it, for you may imagine what a treat it is in this remote spot to listen to music discoursed excellently from a *répertoire* as choice as any in England or elsewhere. The weather, however, is not always auspicious on these occasions. In all mountainous districts sudden variations of temperature are a natural consequence; here they are especially sudden. Without any notice, a cloud will emerge as though from its concealment in the mountains, burst overhead like a squeezed sponge, and discharge itself of its contents with startling rapidity; then how the rain rattles on the shingled roofs and patters at the windows, and streams come rushing down the declivities! You think the day is hopeless, but as suddenly all is serene again, and the sun soon removes all traces of moisture. Then again, at other times, thick mists come charging at you, rolling rapidly down from the hills, and you are quickly enveloped in as pretty a fog as even London could boast of; but this is only vapour, not smoke, and it soon passes away. You may expect these, according to my short experience of the climate, two or three times a day, and so it is a wise precaution never to be unprovided with a waterproof.

The negroes consider themselves admirable weather-prophets, as well as wise in most matters. It pleases them to be consulted, and they always have a decided opinion at your service. "It will rain, sar," or "it will not rain, sar." One day as we were seated at luncheon, the sky became all at once obscured, and there was a low, hollow, moaning sound, which increased to a roaring noise, as though a vast body of water had broken through its dam, and were rushing down the valley. In these lands of earthquakes and hurricanes people are sensitive of convulsions of nature. We rushed outside, but nothing was to be seen, except clouds flying beneath us and over our heads, and the air-currents were so varied that one set of clouds was flying north, and another was being driven south, whilst a third higher up was crossing over the others. However, all passed away, and fortunately nothing came of it. Some black people whom we interrogated accounted for the noise by attributing it to the wind rushing through the valley.

CHAPTER IX.

CATHERINE'S PEAK.—ROPLEY.—COFFEE-WORKS.

Friday, June 12th.—The weather is delightful to-day; in fact, I have not yet found it oppressive. I do not believe that since I have been here the thermometer has ever exceeded 75°. I was amused at hearing of an old quartermaster who, having just arrived out here with his regiment from the land of cakes and mists, was so surprised to see the sun shining on two consecutive days that he made his next morning's salutation to the commanding officer with, "Anither fine day, Cornel!" This afternoon we are to make the ascent of Catherine's Peak, so called (I find in Gardner's "History," p. 129) from the Christian name of the wife of Lieut.-Governor Moore, and a sister of Edward Long, the historian, who was the first lady who ascended the Peak. Previously we were entertained at luncheon in one of the detached huts, which, owing to the military rank of the occupier, happened to be one of the best of them. It is surrounded by a garden, where, amongst other flowers, I noticed a green rose, and a gorgeous hibiscus decorated the porch. A small but prolific kitchen-garden supplies potatoes, lettuces, and other vegetables, which are luxuries here. The field-officers' quarters afford moderate accommodation, but woe betide the captains and subalterns if they are married and have children.

Our gallant host and his handsome wife bade us welcome to a repast which would have done credit to a professed *chef;* at which delicate land-crabs, mayonnaise of cray-fish, chirimoya tart, and a refreshing drink of granadilla seed (like those in the inside of a melon or passion-flower) mixed up with sherry, were among the local characteristics which I remember. Then we started for our climb up the hill: some on horseback, some on foot. We passed the bath-house, and then reached a clump of oaks—the only ones here, I believe. There are some ruins of substantial walls. A great house once stood here, I am told, in the midst of a large sugar plantation; but this, like many others, had been abandoned when the emancipation occurred, and labour could not be procured. Then amidst steep rides cut through the trees, for the hill is wooded up to its peak. At length the path narrowed, the bush thickened, the incline sharpened until we emerged on a little plateau at the summit. We are now 5,000 feet above the level of the sea, and the view is worth the labour of the ascent. You can now apprehend the "crumpled" nature of the country: hills all around, green valleys, most of them with streams running through them, and white villages dotted here and there on the slopes. But the grand feature of all is the "Blue Mountains," which rise towering above all the rest. This ridge is the backbone of the island, extending longitudinally from east to west, here and there intersected by other high ridges traversing it from north to south. Its peak has an elevation of 7,100 feet, the highest point in the island. This is generally obscured by clouds; but we caught occasional glimpses of it. Then we commenced the descent. The path was slippery and stony. I preferred to walk, and generously offered Beethoven's services to any of the pedestrians, but they were declined with thanks, so I led him down behind me. Then we are out in the open again; some magnolia-trees are climbed for their flowers by certain active ones of the party, and, leaving our horses, we hunt for wild strawberries — very small, like Alpines, but without their flavour.

The mountain roads are simply awful: those who ride over them do so at the constant peril of their necks: accidents often occur, sometimes with fatal consequences. They do not deserve the name of roads, being merely bridle paths hewn out on the side of the limestone hills. Macadam, that Colossus of roads, would have been a treasure up here, and would have saved some lives and much disquietude; for lumps of rock stand erect in the way, and when your animal is descending from ledge to ledge with his head pointing over a precipice of some hundred feet, it requires confidence in your horse and self-possession not to check him when he is looking out for a safe place on which to tread. "*Stare antiquas vias*" is all very well in some matters, but in these I am a genuine reformer.

A continual change of the surface, with a disintegration of the exterior edge, is wrought by the heavy rain-falls, and the wear caused by travelling soon destroys the level. This primitive mode of locomotion—so different from our conventional habits—is not without its charm for awhile, and the feeling that it is not devoid of insecurity produces perhaps an additional stimulus.

The horses acquire the habit of proceeding safely in difficult places. Every one keeps a nag of some sort here. They are generally small light things about fourteen hands high. During my many perilous rides, not one of the animals I bestrode ever made a false step. I am only surprised that accidents do not occur more frequently. Six weeks before I arrived, an officer of artillery met with a very serious one, and when I saw the site of the fall I wondered that he was alive—I cannot say to tell the tale, for the shock was so great that he recollects nothing about it. There is one road, the worst of all, called "The Warwickshire," after the 6th Regiment, which constructed it. That gallant corps has not added to its laurels by this achievement, although the pluck of the rider is tested by riding over it, and the Victoria Cross should be the reward for the performance. One day we went along this road to see a candlestick-tree (*Candelabra cereus*), a tree thirty feet high, with branches growing straight upwards. Another day we rode down our hill and up the opposite one to lunch at Ropley. We passed the gates of Craigton, the Governor's country residence, but it was untenanted at the time. Arrived at our destination, the proverbial West Indian welcome and hospitality were extended to us. After an excellent dinner, as in fact it was, we adjourned to the garden, and seating ourselves on the terrace overhanging the valley, we sipped our coffee—you know Jamaica coffee is famous—surveyed the enchanting view, and enjoyed the conversation of some most agreeable people. A learned judge pointed out to me the estate where Bogle (of the Tichborne trial) resided. By-the-bye, I subsequently heard a curious story about this said estate, from an " old inhabitant," to this effect:—

A wild member of the Tichborne family was sent out here as manager of the Mona estate, which belonged at that time to the Duke of Buckingham. Bogle was a lad working on the property, was taken into the service of the manager, and so became acquainted with much concerning the Tichborne family. The manager, so runs the story, left two illegitimate children, one of whom might have been the Claimant.

"I know not how the truth may be,
I tell the tale as 'twas told to me."

Another thing I learnt was undoubtedly true; that an ardent sportsman, a Mr. O'Sullivan, who lived in the mountains above Spanish Town, imported a pack of hounds, but as there was no game for them to hunt, a drag was substituted— a herring, or something of that sort. They met twice a week, but it was found to be poor sport, and they were given up before long. Fancy riding to hounds over this arid country! Mr. O'Sullivan was Provost Marshal, an office of large emoluments in those days; he was also Usher of the Black Rod, bore the mace before the Speaker of the House of Assembly, and a man of good family, and, at one time, of large property. Mr. Sullivan, the present Postmaster-General, is his son, but he has dropped the "O'."

It was so pleasant that we forgot the time, and the misty veil of evening was already spreading around us before we resumed the saddle. Darkness soon overtook us, and I could not see the leading horseman at a few yards' distance. Merely holding the reins, I delegated the responsibility to Beethoven, and he acquitted himself entirely to my satisfaction; and so amidst the evening concert — my steed's great namesake would not have called it symphony — and by the light of the fireflies' lamps, we reached Newcastle in safety.

Wednesday, June 17th.—I had a stiffish walk to-day, for Beethoven, not minding his eye, has scratched it in the stable, and is not available, and we had arranged to view the coffee-works on the Clifton Mount estate. So we passed out below the barracks and turned down the gorge to the left, through which a cascade descends; then up the opposite side—a pretty sharp pull. I kept up, however, with the horses, at the cost of arriving in a state of fusion from the heat. B—— had written to Mr. Maclean, the manager, expressing our wish to be allowed to inspect the works. He met us at the entrance, and how delighted I was when he showed us into his neat sitting-room, with its well-polished floor, and ordered sherry and water to be brought! We then proceeded to view the establishment. First of all, I have collected this information about the cultivation. The plant is raised from the berry, or a sucker—the latter is preferred—five or eight feet square being allowed between each plant. It will thrive in any situation when it is sheltered from the north wind. The best-flavoured fruit is the growth of a warm gravelly mould, or sandy loam, such as forms the slope of the dry red hills of Jamaica. The plant looks like a handsome laurel, powdered in the blossoming season with fragrant white flowers; the berries red and pulpy, like small cherries, and sweet too, which one would not expect. The height of the plant varies from three to ten feet; it lasts several years, being cut down annually after bearing; so that the appearance of a coffee plantation, except in the flowering and fruiting season, is scrubby and neglected, as it requires but little care in cultivation. The average annual produce of one of these plants is one pound of coffee.

Mr. Maclean, who is evidently a very intelligent person, took great pains to explain to us the process of preparing the berries. It seemed simple enough. Each berry contains two corns (sometimes only one, when a curious name is applied to it), wrapped up in two skins. The first process is to get rid of the outer skin: for this purpose the berries are placed in large troughs and forced through metal sieves, the supply being continually brought up from the rear by cogs turned by water power. The corns slide through into other troughs of water, where they are soaked and thoroughly washed, and the skins are caught by the wires. The next process is to place the corns in a circular dry trough, round which a huge wheel faced with copper travels, turned vertically on its trendle by the same water power; this is for the purpose of removing the inner cuticle or parchment, as it is termed, which is of a glutinous character. This being effected, the corns are winnowed thoroughly, and then placed on tables, where the good and bad corns are carefully sorted by hand, and freed from every other substance, then dropped into drawers beneath the tables, and afterwards carried out and exposed to the heat of the sun on barbecues, or broad terraces, to which I have before alluded.

Barbecue is, I find, a term used in the West Indies for dressing a hog whole, by splitting it to the backbone and laying it upon a large gridiron, raised about two feet above a charcoal fire, with which it is also surrounded. This may be described as "going the whole hog." Hence it may have come to be applied to anything spread out to be dried or cured by the action of heat. I cannot discover the derivation of the word, but the process may be derived from the Maroons, who were ardent hunters of wild boars; and it was probably a primitive manner of dressing pork *al fresco*; it appears, moreover, to have been a successful one, for "Monk" Lewis, who was a *gourmet*, and of whom Byron wrote,

> "I would give many a sugar-cane
> M** L** were alive again!"

in his Journal (January 14, 1816), includes it among the delicacies of Jamaica fare:—"Land and sea turtle, quails, snipes, plovers, pigeons, and doves; excellent pork, barbecued pigs, pepperpots, with numberless other excellent dishes, form the ordinary fare; and even the Lord Mayor need not blush to give his aldermen such a dinner as is placed on my table, even when I dine alone."

Pope, in Satire II., addressed to Mr. Bethel, writes :—

> "Oldfield, with more than harpy throat endued,
> Cries, 'Send me, gods! a whole hog barbecued!'"

I now recollect that delightful Tom Ingoldsby uses the expression in "A Lay of St. Gengulphus,". and I never understood till now what it meant :—

> "Now the festive board with viands is stored,
> Savoury dishes be there, I ween;
> Rich puddings and big, a barbecued pig,
> And ox-tail soup in a china tureen."

CHAPTER X.

JAMAICA.

To convince you that I have endeavoured to "improve the occasion," and not to waste the hours of indoor relaxation, I am going to give you a short account of the rise and progress of the island, of which until now I must confess to have been in profound ignorance, like many others as I presume. Be not alarmed, I am not going to write a long history of Jamaica,* but merely a *précis* of memorabilia of what I have been reading in two histories of the island, lent to me by acquaintances out here, namely, Gardner's "History," and Bridge's "Annals of Jamaica."

Jamaica, a name said to be the corruption of an Indian one, Xaymaca, signifying a land of springs,† is the third in magnitude of the West

---

* This has been re-written and amplified, when publication was decided upon.

† *Se non e vero e ben trovato*, inasmuch as Sloane states that there

Indian Islands, which extend from the shore of Florida on the north, to the mouths of the great river Orinoco on the south.

These islands are divided into the Greater and Lesser Antilles, Jamaica being one of the former group. It is situated in the Atlantic Ocean, 4,000 miles south-west of England, and extends from 17° 40′ to 18° 30′ N. latitude, and from 76° 15′ to 78° 25′ W. longitude. It is about 160 miles long and 50 broad, and contains about 400,000 acres, or 6,250 square miles, with a population numbering at the last census (1871) 506,154. Cuba, the largest of all the islands, contains 54,000 square miles, and Hispaniola, the next in size, 30,000.

It was discovered by Columbus during his second voyage to the New World, in May, 1494, and hence dates its introduction into geographical history. In looking at the map one cannot but feel impressed with the belief that all these islands surrounding the Caribbean Archipelago—

---

are in this island eighty rivers running into the sea ("Voyage," &c., vol. i. p. 7). Some again have supposed that Columbus gave it the name of St. Jago, but this was a name bestowed upon it subsequently. Peter Martyr records that the natives called their island Jamaica. "Primam reperit Insulam, quam Incolæ Jamaicam vocant."—*De Christoph. Columb. Navigat. Pet. Mar.*, cap. 98, p. 91. "Isola di Jamaica, che hora i Christiani chiamano di San Jacomo."—*Navig. et Viaggi da G. B. Ramusio*, iii. 195, A.D. 1565.

lying in a bow or semicircle—were, at some remote period of the world's history, part of the continent, the low-lands having subsequently been submerged by some mighty convulsion.

When Columbus, sailing from Cuba, approached the shores of Jamaica on the north side, he is said to have been captivated by the beauty of the prospect, and surprised at the great number of villages with which the country was studded. The compliment, although not undeserved, was by no means trivial, as he was already acquainted with the two fine islands of Cuba and Hispaniola. The landing of the Spaniards was not altogether unopposed; a flotilla of canoes filled with natives brandishing lances of pointed wood, and yelling furiously, sallied forth in hostile array. A few presents delivered to the crew of the leading canoe induced the hostile armada to retire. Columbus landed next day at a place which he named Auracabeza,[*] but not before his boats had been attacked. A few discharges from their crossbows put the Indians to flight; Columbus then took formal possession of the island. He had come hither in the hope of finding gold; that hope was disappointed. The natives subsequently

[*] Now Ora Cabessa Bay. Probably from Span. *aura*, a breeze, and *cabeza*, head or high'land.

came forward and seemed not unfavourably disposed towards him; but he made no long stay; he saw little or nothing of the interior of the island. Being anxious to return to Cuba, he took advantage of a favourable wind and sailed away. The harbour he named Puerto Bueno, now Dry Harbour, and the last place where he touched Gulf of Buentiempo.*

In a month's time Columbus, wishing to proceed to Hispaniola, but being prevented by a continuance of contrary winds, stood across for Jamaica. He completed, or nearly so, the circumnavigation of the island; for nearly a month he continued beating to the eastward along the southern coast. He afterwards reported of its many excellent harbours in terms of admiration, especially of a great bay containing seven islands, and surrounded by numerous villages,† this being evidently the one now known as Old Harbour.

The testimony of the early navigators corroborates the opinion of Columbus, that the natives found on the islands of Cuba, Jamaica, Hispaniola, and Porto Rico, were scions of the same race, differing materially from the Caribbean inhabitants of those Windward and Leeward smaller

* Irving's "History of Columbus," i. 400.
† Ibid.

islands which prolong the great chain of the Antilles to the southern continent, whence this fierce race of cannibals probably passed over. The more gentle people who inhabited the larger islands most likely migrated from the great hive of Mexico, Yucatan and Florida presenting the nearest points from which they would embark.

Peter Martyr, who wrote in 1488, declares that Jamaica was inhabited by a race of Indians more enlightened and benevolent than any that the discoverers had met with elsewhere. In personal appearance they were tall and well-proportioned, with a remarkable scantiness of clothing, and an exceeding fondness for paint and feathers. Their complexion was a sunburnt brown. They dwelt in huts, the sides of which were formed of canes or reeds, and the roofs of palm-trees. They slept in hammocks (*hamac* being the old Indian name) made of twine netted, the twine being manufactured from the cotton, which grew wild in this and other islands, and afterwards dyed in bright colours. Nature supplied food abundantly; very little labour earned for them the gratification of every want. To agriculture, therefore, they resorted but lightly; they merely turned up the herbage of their savannas, drilling the teeming earth with a short stick and sowing maize and cassava. In this garden of Eden fruit-trees grew in wild luxuriance. They were also hunters of the wild animals, and ardent fishermen. They had their light recreations, dancing being the principal one; they also seem to have indulged in smoking. Gonzales Oviedo, who wrote a "General and Natural History of the Indies" in 1535, says that tobacco was indigenous in Hispaniola; and no doubt it was the same in Jamaica, for it was much used by the native Indians, who smoked it from a tube in the shape of the letter Y, the two branches being inserted in their nostrils and the stem placed in the burning leaves. The plant was called *cohiba*, and its present name was derived from *tabaco*, the rude instrument of their enjoyment.* Columbus states that they were provided with canoes, ornamented at the bows and stern with carving, many of them of great size. One, when measured, proved to be ninety-six feet long, and eight broad; hollowed out, doubtless, from one of those magnificent trees which rise like verdant towers amidst the forests of the tropics.

Nothing was heard of Columbus or the Spaniards by the natives of Jamaica for a period of nine

---

* Bridge's "Jamaica," i. App. p. 600.

years. It would have been fortunate for those peaceful and happy islanders had their intercourse with them terminated here. Once again the great navigator revisited the "land of springs." During his fourth and last voyage, having encountered a series of bad weather off the southern coast of Cuba, he was driven to seek shelter in a harbour of Jamaica, which he named Santa Gloria. He did not, however, escape without the loss of two vessels out of his small squadron, and the remaining ones were found to be irreparably damaged. He therefore, on the 24th of June, 1503, ran them ashore in a place still distinguished as Christopher's Cove. The difficulties and distresses which he encountered from the treachery of some of his officers and crew, the malice of Ovando, the Governor of Hispaniola, to whom he had sent for assistance, the means by which he procured provisions and hospitable treatment from the natives, his wonderful patience and presence of mind whilst his body was racked with pain, are well known. He remained here till June, 1504, when the means of returning to Europe were afforded him. It would be gratifying to be certain of the precise spot which that great man so long honoured with his residence.

Two years afterwards he died; his life, no doubt,

shortened by the privations endured and efforts made during this period, his sufferings being aggravated by the ingratitude of the Spanish monarch. After death, the honour refused to him when alive was accorded to him, and a monument was erected to his memory with this inscription :—

> "A Castilla y á Leon
> Nuevo mundo dio Colon."*

Immediately after his death, his eldest son Diego urgently claimed the restitution of the family offices and privileges, which had been unjustly and illegally suspended during the latter years of his father's life. For two years he pressed his suit with fruitless diligence. He then instituted proceedings against the Crown for the recovery of his rights before the Council of the Indies; and to the honour of that body, its decision was unanimously in his favour. It must be stated that he had strengthened his interests by having gained the hand of Maria de Toledo, a niece of Frederic Duke of Alva (grandfather of the celebrated duke of that name), and first cousin of King Ferdinand. Thus was the foreign family

* "To Castile and Leon
Columbus gave a New World."
Columbo was his correct Genoëse name; Colon is the Spanish, and Columbus the Latinised version.

of Columbus grafted on one of the proudest houses of Spain. The King was constrained to acknowledge his rights, and Ovando was recalled from Hispaniola. Thither Diego proceeded with his wife in 1509, and administered the government. Shortly afterwards he dispatched Juan de Esquivel with seventy men to take possession of Jamaica, to hold it subject to his command, and to form a settlement there, on the spot consecrated in a manner by the memory of his father's shipwreck.

It is remarkable that so small a body of Spaniards should have succeeded in gaining possession of the island, in the teeth of the large population which Jamaica undoubtedly had at that time, especially as the first attempt at landing, fifteen years before, had been violently opposed; and that the conduct of the Spanish crews during their year's stay on their shores, however exemplary that of Christopher Columbus had been, was not such as would have led the islanders to desire a permanent acquaintance. However, Diego Columbus, when summoned to Spain to give an account of his government, reported, amongst other matters, that the island of Jamaica had been subjected and brought under cultivation without bloodshed.*

* Herrera, quoted in Irving, iii. App. p. 302.

Herrera, who wrote in 1620, and other Spanish historians, bear testimony to the mild government of Esquivel, although his antecedents did not justify such a character.* Unhappily for Jamaica, he did not live long, and was buried at Sevilla Nueva, the town he had caused to be erected on the site appointed in his instructions, or, as the Spaniards afterwards named it, Sevilla d'Oro, from the splendour and opulence to which it shortly rose. From him, what is now called Old Harbour received its ancient name of Esquivel.

The success which attended the first colonists must have induced the migration of many Spaniards; for two other towns are mentioned as having been in existence, Melilla, which had its name from a town on the coast of Barbary, taken by the Spaniards in 1497, built, as supposed, at Port Sancta Maria; and Oristan, also called after another town in Barbary, and supposed to have been at Bluefields Bay. Of these two settlements no traces survive. Sloane states that Melilla was on the same side of the island as Sevilla, from which it was about eleven leagues distant on the east, and fourteen leagues from it on the south side was Oristan.

Succeeding governors, not profiting by the mild

* See Irving, iii. App. p. 302.

wisdom of Esquivel's policy, seemed rather to vie in cruelty with those Spanish rulers of Hispaniola who, after the death of Diego Columbus in 1526, desolated the island. The wretched natives were then ground to the dust by the iron yoke of a merciless captivity. Their villages were laid waste, their caciques murdered, and their children borne away into hopeless slavery. Such as were even fortunate enough to escape to the mountains, or secrete themselves in the recesses of their forests, lingered out a miserable existence, till death put an end to their sufferings. The history of mankind affords no scene of greater barbarity than that which was exercised in exterminating this innocent and inoffensive people.

"To this day," says Dallas,* "on the mountains of Jamaica, caves are discovered, the ground of which is strewed with human bones, the peculiar development of the skulls proving them to have belonged to the Indians. Shut up in these recesses when driven from the coast, multitudes of the natives doubtless perished by famine, to evade the sword." Sloane was an eye-witness of this. He says, "I have seen many of their bones in caves in the woods, which some people thought were the remains of those who had voluntarily enclosed or

* "Hist. of the Maroons," i. xxvii.

immured themselves to avoid the severities of their masters." *

The golden capital of Jamaica was not destined to last long; but obscurity and mystery hang over the period of its destruction. This seems certain—that it did not gradually decay, but was depopulated while in an unfinished state, long before the English conquest of Jamaica. Sir Hans Sloane, who visited the ruins in 1688, gives a very interesting account of them.† He found the remains of a church and a castle; the former, which he believed to have been unfinished, was built of freestone and brick. He traced a pavement two miles from the church, which gives an idea of the extent of the town. The walls of the fortress, four feet thick, were composed of pebbles and bricks. Two coats-of-arms lay on the ground, one a ducal one, the other that of a count. When the English took the island, the ruins were overgrown with wood, the trunks of some of the trees being sixty feet

---

* Introduction to " Voyage," p. iv.

† The ruins of the Abbey are still to be seen, about two miles from St. Ann's Bay. The Abbot of Sevilla was Suffragan to the Archbishop of St. Domingo, in Hispaniola. The estate on which they stand still bears the name of Seville, and was originally granted to Captain Heming, a favourite officer of D'Oyley; and was till lately in the possession of one of his descendants. Dampier, the English navigator, was overseer or manager of this estate in 1674, before he went again to sea, and took to bucaneering.

in height. Over the west gate of the church, which then stood entire, and beneath a coat-of-arms, was this inscription :—

PETRVS . MARTIR . AB . ANGLERIA . ITALVS . CIVIS .
  MEDIOLANEN .
PROTHON . APOS . HVIVS . INSVLÆ . ABBAS . SENATVS .
  INDICI . CONSILIARIVS .
LIGNEAM . PRIVS . ÆDEM . HANC . BIS . IGNE .
  CONSVMPTAM . LATERICIO .
ET . QVADRATO . LAPIDE . PRIMVS . A . FVNDAMENTIS .
  EXTRVXIT .

[Peter Martyr, of Angleria, an Italian citizen of Milan, Apostolic Prothonotary, Abbot of this island, Counsellor of the Senate of the Indies, first built this edifice of wood, twice destroyed by fire, then of brick and squared stone.]

A site could not have been more happily selected than this for building a town. In immediate proximity with a fine quarry of white freestone, abundance of good water, a fertile soil, the woods filled with a great variety of valuable timber-trees, the sea and rivers stored with fish, a safe and spacious port, and the distance not remote from their island of Cuba.

Sloane learnt from a conversation with an English officer, Colonel Ballard, who was present at the taking of the island, that it was thought by the Spaniards that their countrymen had been cut off by the Indians, and so the church was left unfinished. Moreri* ascribes the capture of Sevilla

* " Dictionnaire Historique," A.D. 1740.

d'Oro to the English, and the probability is that it was overrun by pirates. The native Indians seem to have been utterly incapable of combining, even in self-defence, against the arms and tactical unity of the Spaniards. Indeed, had it been otherwise, there would have been no additional immunity in removing to the interior; moreover, the coast offered the means of escape from inland attack, and there was a strongly fortified place at Sevilla. In 1519, ten years after its settlement, De Garay, the Governor of Jamaica at the time, equipped and sent off an expedition to take possession of some territory on the Main, and he dispatched another in the ensuing year: a proof that the Spanish Government of Jamaica was consolidated, and in possession of resources, both of men and money. All points to the probability that the city was open to predatory attacks over the sea, which accounts for the unfinished state of the buildings, and supplies a reason why its inhabitants should have removed to a central inland situation.

It is certain that, from some adequate cause, Sevilla became suddenly deserted, and this led to the selection of a site remote from the scene of its disasters. This was found on the banks of the Cobre, which flows through a vast savanna, sufficiently distant from the sea to guard against the dangers of surprise, and with a defensible pass in the rear. Thither, about the year 1520, the colonists proceeded, and began their labours afresh. A town quickly arose, which received the name of St. Iago de la Vega (St. James of the Plain), to distinguish it from Santiago de Cuba; St. James being the patron saint of Spain. The English on their arrival renamed it Spanish Town. The new settlement rapidly rose to affluence, and in a few years rivalled the former capital, if not in magnificence, at least in population. An abbey was founded, churches were built, one said to have been styled Church of the Red, and the other of the White Cross, and a square was laid out in the Spanish-American fashion; and the surrounding savannas were converted into a productive district by the labour of a few imported slaves, for the native population was now extinct.

Notwithstanding the supposed security of its position, Sir Anthony Sherley, in Jan. 1596-7, landed on the south coast, marched the six miles to St. Iago, and made an easy conquest of it, and of the whole island. He remained three months, and left bountifully supplied with dried beef and "cassavi meal." He describes the island as being marvellously fertile, and a garden or storehouse for divers parts of the Main.* It was probably after this visit that some measures were taken for the protection of the southern approach to the new capital. A battery called the TWELVE APOSTLES was erected at the entrance to the harbour, opposite to what was afterwards Port Royal; and a fort called PASSAGE FORT at the mouth of the Cobre.

After this incursion, no one thought it worth while to trouble the colony until about forty years afterwards (in the year 1635), when Captain or Colonel William Jackson made a descent upon it. He had collected a force in the Windward Islands, and landed where his predecessor had; but he found the Spaniards prepared to oppose his progress, and a sharp fight ensued at Passage Fort. Being successful, he marched at once to St. Iago, stormed the town, and soon entered it sword in hand. He plundered it of everything valuable, and the Spaniards were glad to offer a certain sum to save the city from being burnt. The Colonel then retired to his ships, but many of his troops deserted, joined the Spaniards, and remained in the island. It appears that the town was fortified at that time: a ditch is traceable which was excavated by the

* Hakluyt's "Voyages," ed. 1600, iii. 601.

Spaniards towards the savanna, and terminated at a bastion flanked with a fortified building, called the Fort House.*

For twenty years after this, the island remained in historical obscurity, and then a new era dawned. Oliver Cromwell turned his attention towards the Spanish possessions in the West Indies. Plausible pretences could be raised in justification, as in most cases of political aggression; but the prospect of reaping, at a small cost, an abundant harvest of wealth and glory, and the opportunity of engaging in foreign service officers and men whose loyalty he mistrusted, were doubtless his real motives.

He prepared an expedition consisting of thirty sail, with 12,000 sailors and 2,500 soldiers, under the joint command of Penn as Admiral, and of Venables as General. The fleet set sail from Portsmouth December 26, 1654, with sealed orders, and proceeded to the English settlements in the West Indies. Many planters, and English, Scotch, and Irish royalists who had been expatriated, were induced to join; so that according to Venables, his force amounted to 6,551 men, of which 1,851 were horse and foot from Barba-

* "Hist. of Jamaica" (A.D. 1774), ii. 31.

does, and 1,600 infantry raised in Nevis, St. Kitts, and Montserrat.

The capture of the rich island of Hispaniola was the object to which the expedition was directed, and thither it proceeded, so soon as the reinforcements were shipped. By the mismanagement of the commanders, the attempt proved an utter failure; many were killed, and the troops had to be re-embarked. Had the fleet at once entered the harbour of St. Domingo, the probability is that the town would have at once surrendered, instead of which the troops were landed forty miles distant—a step entailing ruin on the expedition.

Penn and Venables no doubt felt that something must be done to retrieve the disgrace of the failure; they therefore directed their course to Jamaica.

On the 10th May, 1655,* the British fleet rounded the point of Caguaya, and sailing up

* Bridges and Gardner, in their Histories of Jamaica, assign the 3rd May as the day of landing, but the following extracts decide the date (the variety of spelling Jamaica is curious):—

" 10th May, anchored in the harbour off Jamico."—*Letter from John Daniels* (a Commissary), Thurloe, iii. 505.

" On the 10th came into the harbor of Gemegoe."—*Gregory Butler* (one of the three Commissioners), ibid. 755.

"—The 9th saw Jamaica. The 10th came on shore."—*Penn's Account to the Council*, ibid. iv. 28.

directly to Passage Fort, where nine guns wer mounted, captured it without difficulty, the garrison forsaking it and fleeing to St. Iago to spread the alarm. Venables marched next morning to invest the capital.

Here again was incompetency manifest. He should have marched on the same day, when he could have entered the city, the inhabitants of which were already affrighted by the exaggerated accounts of the fugitives; and the wealth of the place would have been in his grasp. He marched next day, and when in sight of the city he was met by a flag of truce, he consented to retire and to receive commissioners the next day. After six days of inaction, a capitulation was signed. When he entered the city, he found bare walls. The Spaniards had fled; and as they had been afforded ample time to make their arrangements, they were not likely to leave their treasures behind. So the English flag flew over St. Iago de la Vega for the first time; and Jamaica became a possession of England, as it has remained ever since.

Surely the Castilian blood in these colonists' veins must have become sadly diluted, when men who were descendants of that hardy race ot bold adventurers, who had added a new hemisphere to the Spanish dominions, should have made no effort whatever to drive out the invaders. By the terms of the capitulation the lives of all the inhabitants were granted them, and they were free to depart from the island, with the exception of those who had deserted from Jackson.

For one hundred and sixty years the Spaniards had ruled over Jamaica. Of the large native population, which Columbus and others recorded as existing, not a descendant remained. Was the government of the English republicans more paternal?

The Spaniards with their slaves retired to the north side of the island, and the Governor[*] with others went away by sea, promising to return with assistance to expel the English. Those who remained were formed into detached bodies in order to harass the invaders. Gradually, however, the Spaniards left the island, leaving their negroes to hold the mountain fortresses.

The number of the population at the time of the English conquest is variously estimated. Sloane, who wrote only twenty-two years after it, states that "Colonel Ballard, who was pre-

[*] Sloane calls him "Don Juan Ramires de Arellano;" Dallas, "Don Christopher Sasi Arnaldo;" Bridges, "Don Sasi;" and Gardner, "Don Arnoldi Sasi."

sent at the taking of the island, assured me, that the Spaniards (who inhabited the island to the number of 5,000, with as many blacks)," &c.*
Sloane also asserts that St. Iago in the time of the Spaniards consisted of 2,000 houses, four churches, and a monastery.

Grieved at the scanty amount of plunder left for them, and disappointed at discovering no buried treasures, the English Puritans relieved their consciences by gutting and demolishing the churches, and converting the bell-metal into bullets. The fatal effects of mal-organization were now evident. Divided responsibility usually results in disaster. The Admiral and General had proved themselves incompetent, the former not being free from imputations on his courage.† They had no sentiments in common, except that both were royalists at heart, which was probably the reason that three commissioners were appointed to accompany the expedition, invested with powers to control the operations of the commanders. As for the soldiers, according to Venables' account, instead of being selected from the tried veterans of the republic, they were the refuse of the army; ill supplied with arms and

* "Voyage," p. lxvii.
† Pepys' "Diary," ii. 60.

provisions, which latter, in consequence of the want of harmony between the Admiral and the General, were not landed.

A dispatch of Major-General Fortescue to the General, dated about the middle of May, 1655, proves this fact. "According to your order, I sent 400 men, and 60 to fetch up the provisions and ammunition, which Admiral Penn promised should be landed this morning, whereby we might have been enabled to march, according to your order, against the enemy, who still remain refractory, but one of my officers returned from the seaside assures me no provisions were landed when he came away. The soldiers have not had any provisions for almost forty-eight hours, and but one biscuit a man since we came hither."*

A one-biscuit man was not likely to prove a formidable opponent, and no wonder that the enemy became proportionably daring. Parties of English sent out to forage often fell into ambuscades, and the enemy even ventured up to the outskirts of St. Iago, and fired it in several places.

In another month 2,000, or about half the army, were prostrated by sickness. "They die daily, through want of bread and brandy, and the

* Bridge i. 40

survivors look more like dead men crept out of their graves than persons living," wrote Venables.*

The General himself fell sick and sailed for England, and the Admiral not deeming it to his interest that an uncontradicted report of the proceedings of the expedition should be given in his absence, followed him immediately with a portion of the fleet. On their arrival in England, the Protector sent them both to the Tower. Indignant as Cromwell justly was, could the subsequent flourishing position of the hitherto insignificant Jamaica have been foreshadowed, he and the nation might have been consoled. Oliver, however, was not a man to neglect an advantage, however remote. Having expected some more important conquest, he was still determined to make the most of what he had acquired. It appears from the documents in Thurloe that he paid great attention to the sustentation of the West Indian colonies, as affording facilities for future attempts on the Spanish possessions. He issued a proclamation offering liberal terms for the encouragement of settlers in the island, and took active measures to procure additions to their numbers. "Both in England and Scotland," he

* Thurloe, iii. 560. (June 13, 1655.)

wrote, "you will have what men and women we could well transport;" and he verifies his words, for the Council of State voted that "one thousand girls, and as many young men, should be listed in Ireland, and sent over to Jamaica." In November of the same year (1656) Cromwell ordered the Scotch Government to apprehend "all known idle, masterless persons, robbers, and vagabonds, male and female, and transport them to Jamaica."*

Goodson succeeded to the command of the fleet, and Fortescue to that of the army; both energetic officers. The latter soon succumbed to the effects of the climate, and Colonel D'Oyley, the next senior officer, took the command. Of the three commissioners, one returned to England without leave, and the other two shortly afterwards died. The Protector sent out Major Sedgwick in the place of the one who had returned, and he was afterwards ordered to assume the sole direction of affairs, as there were good reasons for mistrusting D'Oyley's fidelity to the republic.

Sedgwick's letters describe the army as being in a deplorable condition. Many of the officers were sick, many were dead, and not a few had left the island. The men having come out with hopes of plunder, and finding none, were dis-

* Long, "History of Jamaica," i. 244.

contented—subjected to the white man's scourge of fever, aggravated by bad food—felt no inclination to settle in the island, although portions of land were offered. A military spirit, fostered during the turbulent times in England, rendered both officers and men dissatisfied with civil inactivity; they envied the reckless lives of the daring freebooters, who were repeatedly bringing in prizes to Caguaya Point, and who lived in revelry and debauchery as long as their gains lasted. A spirit of insubordination, bordering on mutiny, was generated, and to a degree not often exceeded. They not only wantonly and almost entirely destroyed the cattle and swine which had been left in such abundance, but maliciously rooted up the provision grounds which had been prepared by the Spaniards. In short, their conduct seems to have been that of men who hoped that the failure of the settlement might lead to the abandonment of the island. "Such kind of spirit breathing in Englishmen," wrote Sedgwick, "I never met with till now."

The consequence was that a scarcity ensued approaching to famine. Under its pressure, numbers were driven to such extremity, that not only unripe fruit and noxious vegetables, but even snakes and lizards were eagerly devoured

Disease followed, and the mortality was so great that carcasses lay unburied in the bushes and on the highways.

The navy seems to have enjoyed a remarkable exemption from sickness, as well as from the disaffection which pervaded the army. All the work of the colony was performed by the seamen, while the soldiers looked on sullenly.

The Spanish Government was goaded on unwillingly to declare war against England. Some effort for the recovery of Jamaica was to be anticipated, and Cromwell warned Goodson that "a goodly force" might be expected from that quarter. Passage Fort was therefore strengthened, and a battery, mounting twenty-one guns, was erected at Caguaya Point.

The Protector, being apprised of the state of affairs in the colony, exerted himself with his usual vigour to afford relief. He dispatched supplies of every description. Colonel Humphrey (whose father had borne the sword before Bradshaw, at the trial of Charles I.) arrived with his regiment of 850 men, but within a few weeks not one-third remained fit for duty. Sedgwick bore up bravely against the disasters and difficulties that surrounded him, but he fell a victim to the fatal climate, and his administration of eight months was brought to a close on the 24th of June, 1656. The reins of government were again in D'Oyley's hands, but the Protector sent out General Brayne, late Governor of Lochaber, as successor to Sedgwick. He found disease, distress, and confusion everywhere, and he set vigorously to work to remove the causes of evil. Finding that some of the officers prevented their men from engaging in agriculture, he removed them from the island. By judicious management, small holdings of land were cultivated successfully, and soldiers were hired to till the soil. But it was found that a tropical climate was ill adapted for the outdoor toil of Europeans. Brayne, therefore, applied to the Protector for an importation of African slaves, enforcing his plea by the argument that, as their masters would have to pay for them, they would feel a greater interest in the preservation of their lives than in that of hired labourers, and, therefore, more careful to work them with moderation.

Whilst the new Governor was busily engaged in endeavouring to improve the condition of the colony, military precautions were not neglected. The fortifications on the southern coast were strengthened; companies of the regiments were consolidated, and a certain number of men always kept under arms. Parties were dispatched against the predatory bands which still harassed the settlers; and the prisoners who were made confirmed the expectation of the speedy arrival of a rescuing force of Spaniards.

"Port Royal," says Gardner (p. 43), "was founded by Brayne; Caguaya was the name given to the spot by the Spaniards." Did he not enlarge or remodel it? There was already a town there. In the articles of capitulation, all persons wishing to leave the island were required to present themselves "upon the savanna before the town of Caguaya."* Point Cagway, as it was familiarly called by the English, and in a map of Jamaica according to a survey made in the year 1670,† the present KINGSTON HARBOUR is set down as CAGWAY HARBOUR. The name is not Spanish, and, therefore, probably Indian. It has been suggested that the name may be derived from Caragua, the Brazilian name of the Coratoe, or great American aloe, which grows in abundance thereabouts. Sloane, however, in his "Natural History," does not allude to this circumstance.

* Bridges, i. 401.
† Published in a "History of Jamaica," 1774. (A valuable work, the author of which has not prefixed his name.)

Brayne's useful career in the island was of very little longer duration than that of his predecessor. Within ten months he was buried, with as much pomp as affairs would admit of, at Spanish Town. His demise invested D'Oyley temporally with the supreme command for the third time. This brave officer, possibly anticipating another abrupt supersession, addressed a letter to the Protector requesting to be recalled. Cromwell, however, either by a tardy appreciation of his merits, or experiencing a difficulty in providing a successor after the fatality that had attended the Governors, confirmed his succession.

It was not long before his military qualities were brought into requisition. Spain could not see so valuable a gem torn from her diadem without a wish to replace it, and its recapture became, towards the end of 1657, an object of great national concern. Its defenceless state, the dissatisfaction of the English troops, and the exertions making by Oliver Cromwell to afford them relief as well as to augment their numbers, induced the belief that the time had arrived for retrieving the honour of the country by the restoration of the island to the Spanish crown. In May, 1658, Don Christopher Arnoldi Sasi, the ex-Governor of Jamaica, landed on the north side of the island at Ocho Rios Bay, and thirty companies of Spanish infantry arrived shortly after, and disembarked at Rio Nuevo Bay. Measures were also taken to unite the scattered bands of negroes and Spanish fugitives.

In consequence of the scanty means of communication with the north of the island, it was some days before the intelligence of the landing reached D'Oyley, of which time the Spaniards made good use, by entrenching themselves and erecting a strong redoubt. Moreover, it was necessary to convey the English force by sea; for to advance across the country was impossible, the interior being little known; the track across the mountains was not practicable for heavy baggage or artillery, and ambuscades could be easily planned by the enemy, to whom the fastnesses were familiar.

On the 11th of June, D'Oyley set sail from Caguaya with 750 picked men, and eleven days were occupied in the voyage. A flag was sent to summon the rightful owners of the island to surrender, which, of course, they declined to do. The British troops were then landed, and after a vigorous assault the redoubt was taken, and the Spaniards were driven from every position, upwards of 400 being killed, and more than 100 taken prisoners, together with colours, guns, and ammunition, and a plentiful supply of wine and other provisions, most gladdening to the hearts of the victors. The English loss was inconsiderable—4 officers and 23 private men killed. The victory was attended with important results: it served to wipe away the disgrace of St. Domingo, and it impressed the Spanish commanders with profound respect for British valour, so that a fleet about to bring reinforcements changed its destination, and left the fugitives to their fate. Most of these made their escape over the sea. The roving negroes still continued troublesome, by encouraging slaves to rebel or to desert; some few joined the English, and assisted in the capture of their fellows, but the majority assuming the character of wild banditti, and being from time to time reinforced by more fugitive slaves, became the nucleus of that body of independent occupants of the interior, subsequently known as Maroons, who—too weak to conquer, yet strong enough to injure—were for many succeeding years the pests of the island.

Once again Don Christopher made an effort to recover possession of the island which had so long been the home of Spaniards. D'Oyley sent Colonel Tyson with a detachment of soldiers and a party of his new negro allies against him. Tyson found him posted with a small force of 133 men on the hill above San Cheireras, drove him out of his position, and pursued him to the seaside, from whence he escaped in a canoe. The spot of the conflict is marked in the grounds of Shaw Park by a piece of heavy ordnance, and the harbour from which he embarked still retains the name of Runaway Bay.*

The two following Jamaica orders, quoted by Montgomery Martin,† afford a curious picture of the manners of the times :—

"August, 14, 1656.—An order signed Edward D'Oyley, for distribution to the army of 1,781 Bibles."

"August 26, 1659.—Order issued this day unto Mr. Peter Pugh, Treasurer, to pay unto John Hoy the sum of twenty pounds sterling, out of the impost money, to pay for fifteen dogs, bought by him for the hunting of the negroes."

Under the shadow of D'Oyley's power, Jamaica increased in prosperity. Secure in their properties, the settlers applied themselves to the improvement of them, and cultivation was rapidly extended. Caguaya became the mercantile dépôt of the West, the chief place of resort for privateers, and the grand repository of their prizes and plunder. The exploits of the association of

---

* Bridges, i. 239.
† "British Colonies," iii. 146.

pirates, under the name of Bucaneers, form one of the most remarkable episodes in the history of the seventeenth century.

It is stated that they derived their origin from a band of Frenchmen, who sought to settle themselves on the island of St. Christopher, one of the Antilles. Driven thence, some of them fled to the western coast of St. Domingo, others to the small island of Tortuga, on the north-west coast of St. Domingo, several Englishmen, led by a similar roving disposition, having associated themselves. The fugitives of St. Domingo employed themselves chiefly in the chase of the wild cattle which abounded there. The hides were sold to the trading vessels that visited the coast, and the flesh was cured in a peculiar manner, which they learnt from the natives, and called *Boucan* in Indian phraseology. From this word the French adapted the verb *boucaner*, "to dry red, without salt."* Hence comes the noun Boucanier, and our Bucaneer.

These hunters lived in the rudest state of nature, sharing in common all that they could make or take. The Spaniards, who could not apprehend them, determined to extirpate the cattle in the island, so as to deprive these adventurers of the

* "Dictionnaire de Trevoux."

means of sustenance, in order that they might be driven to seek their living elsewhere. Had they been left alone, possibly they might gradually have settled down into quiet, industrious communities, although not the choicest representatives of their respective nationalities. But Spain, in right of her priority of discovery, and the subsequent bull of Pope Alexander VI. (May 2, 1493), considered the whole of the New World as treasure-trove, of which she was the lawful and exclusive mistress. Every foreigner found among the islands or on the coast of America was treated as a smuggler and robber; and this being the case, it is no wonder that these adventurers became so, and returned cruelty by cruelty. The exaggerated accounts of the boundless wealth of the New World aroused the desires of the needy and enterprising, who flocked thither chiefly from the seaports of the Northern European nations, the preponderance being English and French, undismayed by the reports of Spanish atrocities.

> "Quid non mortalia pectora cogis,
> Auri sacra fames?"

To repress these interlopers, the Spanish employed *guarda-costas*, the commanders of which were instructed to massacre all their prisoners. This tended to produce a close alliance, offensive and defensive, among the mariners of all other countries, who in their turn made descents on the coasts, and ravaged the weaker Spanish towns and settlements, and there can be little doubt that Sevilla d'Oro owed its depopulation to them. A permanent state of hostilities was thus established in the West Indies, entirely independent of the existence of peace or war at home. These "Brethren of the Coast," knowing what they had to expect, were always prepared to fight desperately, and their name in turn became allied with bravery and brutality. Recruited as they were from all classes and diverse nations, yet none but the reckless would be likely to join the association.

> "Nor swelling seas, nor threatening skies
> Prevent the pirates' course :
> Their lives to selfish ends decreed,
> Through blood and rapine they proceed.
> No anxious thoughts of ill-repute
> Suspend the impetuous and unjust pursuit ;
> But power and wealth obtained, guilty and great,
> Their fellow-creatures' fears they raise, or urge their hate."
>
> CONGREVE.

As they increased in numbers, so also they resolved on more daring enterprises with an intrepidity which bade defiance to danger. Their efforts were especially directed against the Spanish "Plate fleets" as they were termed, which sailed from Europe laden with the treasures of the West.

Although lawless marauders, they instituted a code of laws, maintained with the honour which the lowest reprobates are reputed to possess amongst themselves, such as an equal distribution of plunder and a community of goods. A false oath was rare, and its occurrence was punished rigorously. In some instances religion was strangely mingled with their vices. In victualling their ships they considered purchase degrading to their profession :—

> " The good old rule
> Sufficed them—the simple plan,
> That they should take, who have the power,
> And they should keep—who can."

The wealth which they acquired was quickly spent in gambling and debauchery. When Jamaica fell into the hands of the English, the bucaneers made Caguaya their rendezvous. Secure from attack, they could here expose their plunder, and dissipate *ad libitum*. They were welcomed by all there as enemies of the Spaniards. The governors hailed them as auxiliaries, and employed them to pursue the fugitive Spaniards and negroes on account of their experience in irregular warfare. The settlers rejoiced at their appearance, as creating a ready mart for inland produce paid for at a prodigal rate, and the unsettled gazed with admiration at the hardy sea-rovers, and offered to enlist in their service. A flood of wealth was poured into the island, and rich cargoes were piled upon the shores of Caguaya. Every refinement of luxury was placed within reach, and gratification afforded to the most degraded vice. The pirates were thus in a very short time reduced to poverty, and often to the extremities of distress, until fresh spoil made them heroes again.

The effect of the contamination of such men, and the recurrence of such scenes, is obvious; the character of the white population of the colony at this period is stated to have been deplorable. But on the other side it must be recorded that to them we may owe the possession of Jamaica, for it can hardly be supposed that the Spaniards would have relaxed in their efforts to retake the island—especially when the English means of internal defence were at first notoriously feeble—unless they had been checked by the attacks of whole squadrons of privateers, which obliged them to retain their fleets to defend their valuable possessions elsewhere.

Nor were the lives of these desperadoes altogether unproductive of advantage, independently of the wealth which they poured into Jamaica, for without being aware of the importance of their communications, they were continually contributing information of the sources of wealth, the local peculiarities, the political positions, the manners and customs, the nature of the soil, and the productions of those countries which they infested; and although they are branded with the general name of pirates, they acted either with the sanction or connivance of their Governments, otherwise they would not have ventured as they did to sojourn in the harbour of Jamaica, and when England wished to make reprisals on Spain, many of them obtained commissions or letters of marque, and acted as accredited privateers.* This gave a colour of legitimacy and honour to their calling, and confounded the notions of right and wrong in ignorant minds.

Those reckless Filibusters were the men of their times, and the fathers of our national vigour and prosperity. Among them were some whose achievements were equal to those of any of the most eminent warriors of historic fame; their renown is to this day

* "Sir William Beaston mentions that, in 1668, during Sir Thomas Modiford's government, who, by his own sole authority, had twice proclaimed war against the Spaniards, the King (Charles II.) sent out the *Oxford* frigate, which brought instructions to countenance the war, and empowering him to commission whatever persons he thought good *to be partners* with his Majesty in the plunder, *they finding victuals, wear, and tear;* so that his Majesty entered very seriously into the privateering business, and held this reputable partnership for some years."—*Beaston's Journal*, in Leenan's "Jamaica Tracts," p. 284.

echoed by traditionary tales, told and credited in every island of the West Indies. A prestige of bravery attached itself to the name of British sailors, which perhaps served as a stimulus to those dashing acts of temerity which characterized the future Royal Navy of Great Britain.

CHAPTER XI.

JAMAICA (*continued*).

ON September 3rd, 1658, Oliver Cromwell closed his eventful career. His son and successor Richard was not equal to the responsibilities and dangers of the Government at home; it is therefore not surprising that little or no attention was paid to the distant colonies. Charles II. mounted the throne on May 29th, 1660, but exactly twelve months elapsed before any communication from him reached his subjects in Jamaica. During this interregnum D'Oyley was fully occupied. Although he had conquered the foreign foe, the internal peace of the island was continually disturbed by the partisans of the rival dynasties. Many republicans had resorted thither of late, foreseeing a re-establishment of the monarchy, and apprehending retribution. Among these were Daniel Blagrove* and Colonel Thomas Wayte. A son

---

* His descendants continued to reside in the island until a recent period. The late Mr. John Blagrove, of Cardiff Hall, near St. Ann's

of Thomas Scot—one of Charles's judges—who was executed in 1660, subsequently arrived and settled the plantation called Y. S., in the parish of St. Elizabeth.* Others again there were who argued that as the island had been captured by Cromwell, Charles would now restore it to Spain, in order to be on good terms with that country. The planters desired a civil government, and the soldiers, kept under military discipline without pay, naturally became discontented. It was a trying time for the Governor, but by stringent measures he preserved his authority. It was not then strange that he countenanced the bucaneers, to counterpoise the power and overawe the tur-

---

Bay, was an eminent agriculturist, and a person of much consideration. He died in 1824, and was buried at Titchfield, Hants. On his large Jamaica estates he owned about 1,500 slaves, to whom he was a most kind master, and who were specimens of the happiness and comfort to which a slave population may attain. They appear to have repaid his care and affection. Mr. Blagrove left a legacy to them which speaks for itself:—" And, lastly, to my loving people—denominated and recognised by law as, and being, in fact, my slaves in Jamaica, but more estimated and considered by me and my family as tenants for life attached to the soil—I bequeath a dollar for every man, woman, and child, as a small token of my regard for their faithful and affectionate service, and willing labours to myself and family, being reciprocally bound in one general tie of master and servant in the prosperity of the land, from which we draw our mutual comfort and subsistence," &c.

* A daughter of his married one of the Beckford family; her father, being a royalist, had been compelled to fly from England during the Commonwealth.

bulence of the republican portion of the settlers and soldiery. Two officers were sentenced to death by court-martial, one being Tyson, who had acted so ably against the Spaniards, and order was partially restored.

In this state of suspense, on May 29th, 1661, the first anniversary of the Restoration, the *Diamond* frigate arrived, and brought a commission from the King to D'Oyley, confirming him in the government of the island, with orders that the army should be immediately disbanded, and a militia formed. A Council of twelve persons was to be appointed, who were empowered to make laws, provided they were not repugnant to those of England, to constitute civil courts, and direct the military forces.* He was further directed to

---

* The following sums were paid to the garrison of Jamaica at its discharge in October, 1662.—*History of Jamaica*, 1774, i. 614.

	£	s.	d.
To the regiment quartered in Liguanea, commanded by Col. Samuel Barry	2,652	5	7
To ditto at Port Royal, Morant, and Yallahs, late D'Oyley's, now Col. Thomas Lynch's	2,582	4	1
To ditto at Guanaboa and Precinct, late Barrington's, now Col. Cornelius Burrough's	2,840	12	6
To ditto at Spanish Town, Angelo, Passage Fort, Old Harbour, and parts adjacent, late Col. Philip Ward's, now Col. Thomas Ballard's	2,671	3	0
	10,746	5	2
To the troop of horse commanded by Captain Robert Nelson	1,527	15	0
	£12,274	0	2

discourage drunkenness and debauchery, and to maintain the Protestant religion according to the order of the Church of England; to complete the fortifications at Caguaya, to encourage planters, and allot and register lands.*

According to his instructions he assembled, as soon as possible, the principal planters and chief officers, and having read aloud his commission, he proclaimed Charles II. as King at Caguaya, which has ever since been called Port Royal to commemorate the event. Thus Jamaica became formally enrolled amongst the possessions of the British Crown.

A civil government was not suitable to D'Oyley's tastes. He expressed a wish to be relieved, and he was informed that Lord Windsor might shortly be expected to arrive as his successor. The preserver of the colony departed apparently unregretted.

The brief sojourn of Windsor in the island may almost be comprised in the well-known words, "Veni, vidi, vici." Two or three months' residence were sufficient to disgust him with tropical life, but in order to achieve something before resignation, he organized an attack upon St. Iago de Cuba, which was successful. Immediately after the return of the expedition, having doubtless

* App. "Journals," House of Assembly.

secured his share of the spoil, and leaving Sir Charles Lyttleton, who had come out with him, as Lieutenant-Governor, and without waiting to review the militia which had now been organized, he sailed for England, affording the babbling Pepys something to trouble his head about and record in his "Diary."* Windsor had been the bearer of a Royal Proclamation, in which every encouragement was offered to agriculturists and settlers. By it, all free persons were permitted to transport themselves, their families and goods (except coin and bullion), to Jamaica, from any part of the British dominions; and their children born in Jamaica were declared entitled to the same privileges as if they had been born in England; and that thirty acres of improvable land shall be granted and allotted to every such person, male or female, being twelve years old or upwards, who now resides, or within two years next ensuing shall reside, within the island; and the Governor was instructed to call an Assembly, to be indifferently chosen by the people at large, to pass laws for their internal government; 100,000 acres of land were to be set apart in each of the four quarters of the island as a royal demesne. He

---

* February 13th, 1662-3.

also brought out an official mace and a great seal for the colony.*

In 1662, Charles II. granted by letters patent to the Duke of York and other distinguished persons a lease of the exclusive right as a Royal Company of Adventurers to trade with Africa. This Company undertook to supply 3,000 slaves annually to the West Indies.

The first recorded census in Jamaica, taken seven years after its capture, namely, in 1662, gives 2,600 white men, 645 women, 408 children, and 552 negroes.†

* "This mace," according to Bridges, i. 424, "cost £80; and the great seal, which was of silver, represented the king seated on his throne, two Indians on their knees presenting fruits, and two cherubim aloft supporting a canopy; and, beneath, the motto:

'DURO DE CORTICE FRUCTUS QUAM DULCIS.'

On the exergue, 'Carolus Secundus, Dei gratiâ Angliæ, &c., et Dominus Jamaicæ.'

"The motto, 'Indus uterque serviet uni,' below a cross *gules*, charged with five pine-apples in a field *argent*, supported by two Indians plumed and condaled (*sic*) (? *condalium*, Lat., a sort of ring which slaves wore), the crest an alligator, and orbicular inscription:

'ECCE ALIUM RAMOS PORREXIT IN ORBEM
NEC STERILIS EST
CRUX.'

"The seal is said to have been designed by the Archbishop of Canterbury." This must have been William Sancroft, whose English composition was jeered at by the Jacobites (Macaulay, ii. 611); his Latin does not seem to have been any better.

† Bridges, i. 427.

Pursuant to the terms of the Royal Proclamation, the Lieutenant-Governor convened the first Legislative Assembly in January, 1664. It consisted of thirty members and a Speaker, who enacted laws which received the sanction of the King. Its sittings were divided between the seat of Government and Port Royal, for the convenience of the public.

To guard against external foes, Fort Charles was commenced, and guns were mounted to protect more fully the rising town of Port Royal. At home, the Maroon negroes, though comparatively few in number, virtually kept possession of the centre of the island, and did not spare a single white man who attempted to form a settlement in the interior. Lyttleton tried conciliation, offering twenty acres of land and freedom to all who would surrender. But the Maroons were already free as the birds of the forest, and had thousands of acres of the richest land in the colony; so these terms offered no inducement. Military coercion was then attempted, but without any successful result.

In May, 1664, Lyttleton returned to England. Shortly after his arrival in Jamaica, he lost his first wife;* a flat stone in the chancel of the Cathedral at Spanish Town, bearing the date of

* His second was "La belle Temple." (See Grammont's "Memoirs.")

January, 1662, marks her resting-place. He was succeeded in the government by Sir Thomas Modiford, a rich planter and late Governor of Barbadoes. He inaugurated some active measures against the Dutch, and his administration was marked by a series of depredations against the Spaniards.

In June, 1671, a treaty of peace being signed with Spain, it was thought desirable to recall Modyford. He was actually sent home as a prisoner, and confined in the Tower; but this was simply a blind. In 1675 he was back in Jamaica as Chief Justice. Four years after he died, and his monument at Spanish Town records that he was "the soule and life of all Jamaica, who first made it what it now is."

Sir Thomas Lynch was the next Governor, and it seems a strange commentary on the professed desire of the English Government to put down piracy, that he should have been succeeded by Henry Morgan, the gallant bucaneer, who had been knighted in recognition of his successful raid at Panama.

On the 13th of April, 1685, the news of the death of Charles II. was communicated to the Council by the Earl of Carlisle, the Governor. The Assembly was in consequence dissolved, and the inhabitants waited, with some anxiety, to learn into whose hands the management of affairs would be committed by the new sovereign. In the meantime, there was trouble in the colony, for the first outbreak of any importance happened among the negro slaves; it was soon suppressed, but in 1686 one of a more sanguinary character occurred in the parish of Clarendon.*

In August, 1687, Christopher, second Duke of Albemarle, left London to assume the government of Jamaica.† Being entirely ruined in fortune, he had been persuaded by certain speculators to join in partnership with them, for the purpose of raising a Spanish galleon sunk near the island. In order to facilitate their proceedings he procured himself to be made Governor of Jamaica. He was accompanied by his duchess, and in his suite was Dr. Sloane, his physician, afterwards the well-known Sir Hans.

The adventure was successful; and the Duke's share amounted, according to Evelyn's belief, to £50,000;‡ it was asserted by others to have reached £90,000. He, however, did not live long enough to reap the benefit of it, for he died next year, and

* Gardner, p. 69.

† "The Duke of Albemarle goes out next week to Jamaica, having £25,000 more paid him for the king, in consideration of his equipage, service in the West (of England), and other arrears."—*Ellis Correspondence*, i. 318.

‡ "Diary," June 6th, 1687.

his body was embalmed and brought to England. His government was highly unpopular. Possessed of no religious principles of his own, he was quite prepared to carry out those of that religion which his sovereign was endeavouring to thrust upon the people of Great Britain. A number of convicts reserved for transportation by Judge Jeffreys after Monmouth's rebellion, had arrived at the colony, and these unfortunates were not likely to receive mercy from Albemarle, who had been the first to take active measures against the rebels.

In 1687 a post-office was first established in Jamaica. The inhabitants, however, could not congratulate themselves on the means of rapid inland transit, inasmuch as, and for several years afterwards, the mails were dispatched only once a week from Kingston, so that a letter sent by this conveyance to no very distant point, Savannah-la-Mar, could not be answered before twelve days. In these days of cheap postage, it is curious to compare the rates from Jamaica to Great Britain, per Act 9 Anne, c. 10:—

	s.	d.	
Single	1	6	sterling
Double	3	0	,,
Treble	4	6	,,
Ounce	6	0	,,

being six times more than the present charge.

The Earl of Inchiquin, who came out as Governor in 1690, brought instructions from William III., directing him to send back to England the convicts who had been condemned for complicity in Monmouth's rebellion. Being a man of ungovernable passions, he was at continued variance with the Assembly till his death in January, 1692.

A variety of disastrous events had occurred in rapid succession. In 1689 a violent hurricane caused great damage to houses, ships, and crops. In 1690 a dangerous servile outbreak distressed the colonists, which, after some effusion of blood, was suppressed by the militia.

This rebellion was not the only element of anxiety; a foreign foe menaced the coasts; for war having been declared against France, her cruisers were seeking opportunity to make incursions wherever practicable. Matters bore a formidable aspect; for there were sympathizers in the island, adherents of James II., who maintained allegiance to him as their rightful sovereign, and disclaimed any to William of Nassau. Bucaneers took advantage of the state of affairs, and plundered the north side of the island. They were actually engaged in this work under a noted leader called Daviot, when the shock of an earthquake alarmed them, and they betook themselves to their boats, but the sea suddenly became so agitated that many of these were swamped and their crews drowned. Those who escaped are said to have been subsequently captured by the British cruisers; and this was the solitary advantage derived from that awful visitation; for it was The Great Earthquake (as it has been termed) of the 7th of June, 1692, when the entire island was shaken through its breadth and length.

A sultry morning dawned without a cloud visible above the horizon, or a breath of air abroad. At 11.40 A.M. there was a gentle tremulous movement of the ground; this was succeeded by another more violent agitation, accompanied with a hollow rolling noise, mysteriously sounding in the earth and air. This dreadful warning, too familiar to West Indian ears, was immediately followed by a third tremendous shock. Screams of anguish and cries of horror which arose were quickly drowned by the rush of waters and the simultaneous crash of falling edifices. In less than three minutes the gay, dissolute, rich, and populous town of Port Royal was a scene of desolation and utter ruin. Of the fifteen hundred houses, which Sloane recorded as existing in his time, not two hundred were left. Solid wharfs loaded with merchandise, massive fortifications, the church, with all the streets next to the shore, sank to the bottom of the sea, the ruins of which are even yet visible. The harbour appeared in motion as if agitated by a storm, yet no wind was stirring; mighty waves rose up and fell with such violence, that ships broke from their anchors, and the *Swan* frigate was forced over the tops of sunken houses, affording a refuge for many of the drowning people. Two thousand people (some accounts say three thousand) perished by the effects of this earthquake.

Far and wide the calamity made itself known. Opposite, at Port Henderson, the shock rent many caverns, still apparent; through these the water, forced up to a high elevation, continued gushing with sulphureous steam for many days. At Passage Fort not one house was left standing. The houses in Spanish Town were shaken to their foundations, the walls of all were split. On the road to Sixteen-mile-walk, two mountains fell and met; the fissures in the hills were closed with colossal masses of disjointed rock, which dammed up the bed of the river, and which, in some places, remain to this hour eternal witnesses of that day's convulsion. The water thus confined rose to an overwhelming height, and bursting its barrier, bore all before it. There was scarcely a mountain on the island that did not change its outline, or a rock which was not rent. For three weeks the shocks were repeated, though with decreasing violence.

The surviving inhabitants of Port Royal, who sought a refuge in temporary huts, where Kingston now stands, were further afflicted by a pestilence, occasioned by the number of dead bodies which floated about the harbour. The malignant fever which ensued caused almost as many deaths as the earthquake. One loss is still severely felt, that of all the official documents and records of the island, a disaster rendering its early history obscure and incomplete.

A marvellous case of preservation during the earthquake is recorded on a tomb existing at Green Bay, on the opposite side of the entrance to the harbour, over against Port Royal. The inscription is still legible, beneath a shield bearing a cock between two mullets in chief, and in base a crescent, with the motto—

"DIEU SUR TOUT.
Here lyeth the body
of
LEWIS GALDY, ESQUIRE,
who departed this life at Port Royal,
the 22nd of December, 1736,
aged 80 years.

" He was born at Montpellier in France ; but left that country for his religion, and came to settle in this island ; where he was swallowed up in the Great Earthquake in the year 1692; and, by the providence of God, was, by another shock, thrown into the sea, and miraculously saved by swimming, until a boat took him up. He lived many years in great reputation, beloved by all who knew him, and much lamented at his death."

The first act of the legislature, on re-assembling, was to appoint the anniversary of that awful visitation as a solemn fast-day. The inhabitants had scarcely time to breathe afresh, when they were menaced by the calamities of war. Intelligence was received that Jamaica was soon to be invaded by the French from Hayti. Prompt measures were taken thereupon by Sir William Beaston, who was administering the government. Martial law was proclaimed; the fortifications of Port Royal were repaired, and some new ones extemporised; the narrow pass east of Kingston, where Rock Fort now stands, was put into a state of defence, some outlying and indefensible places abandoned, and Old Harbour and Carlisle Bay hastily fortified.

On Sunday, the 17th June, 1694, the expected fleet appeared off the coast, under the command of Admiral du Casse, Governor of Hayti. For a month the work of plunder went on, not only on the east, but also on the north coast, accompanied with acts of great cruelty and wanton destruction of property, and about 1,300 negroes were captured. These parts were almost denuded of troops, for the militia had been withdrawn to defend Port Royal. On the 19th July a body of 1,500 French landed in Carlisle Bay; they were opposed by about 200 militia, and some negroes. These, after a gallant resistance, were forced to retreat; but, at the critical moment, four other companies of militia, with a body of horse, arrived, and, although exhausted by a march of thirty miles, fell upon the enemy with such impetuosity, that he was forced to fall back. After three days' skirmishing, the English having collected a force of 700 men, drove the French to their ships with considerable loss, who then gave up the contest, and sailed back to Hayti. In 1702 "the brave old Benbow"—the hero of so many sailors' songs—with his squadron fell in with that of the French under Du Casse. For five days the gallant English Admiral sustained a most unequal contest, being almost entirely unsupported by his captains; on the last day his ship was left to bear the brunt of the fight alone; but, notwithstanding that his leg had been shattered by a chain-shot, he remained on the quarter-deck and continued the engagement, but the enemy effected his escape. When he returned to Jamaica he caused a court-martial to assemble;

one captain was cashiered and imprisoned, and two were sent home and shot at Plymouth. Their conduct resulted not from cowardice, but from dislike of the Admiral, who was a rough seaman, perhaps an overbearing officer of the school which Smollett—himself a surgeon's mate in the Royal Navy—drawing from the life, has in "Roderic Random" and "Peregrine Pickle" made familiar to us.*

To the effects of the earthquake Kingston owed its existence. In 1693 the planning of the town was intrusted to Colonel Lilly, and he designed it according to his military tastes, rather than with any regard to elegance. It was in the form of a parallelogram, one mile in length, and half a mile in width, traversed regularly by streets and lanes, intersecting each other at right angles, except in the upper or north part of the town, where there is a large square.

Port Royal, however, began to rise again in eminence, the great advantage of its situation attracting inhabitants as the popular fears subsided. The war with France gave rise to a system of privateering which poured treasures into it, surpassing even the most brilliant days of the bucaneers.

* Smollett's "History of England," i. 470. See also "Life of Smollett," p. 19.

It continued to increase in size and wealth till the year 1703, when the devoted town was again destroyed, this time by fire. But what the earthquake and conflagration had spared was nearly demolished by a violent hurricane on the 28th August, 1722; and the seat of commerce was finally transferred to Kingston.

In 1728 Sir Nicholas Lawes, who had been Governor, introduced the coffee-plant into Jamaica, the berries, it is said, having been brought from St. Domingo, and planted at his estate at Temple Hall, in St. Andrew's.* He had been succeeded in 1722 by the Duke of Portland, who was accompanied by Colonel Dubourgay, as Lieutenant-Governor, to whom a salary of £1,000 a year had been promised; but as this was an office never hitherto paid during the residence of a Governor, it was considered properly to be an innovation, and the House of Assembly refused to grant it, except for one year, and then only to defray his return passage to England.† The Duke was, however, well received, and his stipend fixed at £5,000 per annum, double what had formerly been given. He became very popular; his hospitality was unbounded; and he probably would have

* Leenan's " Hort. Jamacensis," i. 226.
† Journals, vol. ii. pp. 456—461. Quoted in Gardner, p. 114.

reconciled the differences that existed between the local legislature and the home Government, had he not died suddenly in 1726. His name is perpetuated in the parish of Portland, which was settled during his administration, and the chief village Titchfield was so designated after his second title.

For some years past the island had been kept in a state of alarm by the guerrilla warfare and system of plunder maintained by the Maroons. There were at this time 80,000 negroes in Jamaica, and 8,000 whites.* The term Maroon had hitherto been confined to the body of original Spanish fugitives; and it was not till about the year 1730, when a negro, called Cudjoe, had become formidable as a leader, that he and his people were included in the appellation.† They began at that time to pursue a more regular and connected

* Gardner, 117.
† Edwards ("History of the West Indies," iii. 304) gives the etymon *marráno* on the authority of Long, the historian of Jamaica. *Marráno*, the Spanish substantive, is "a hog;" *marráno*, adjective, is "wild." The Maroons were great hunters of the hog, and were themselves as wild as that animal, so either would apply; but it is more probably derived from the Spanish *cimarrón*, wild, unruly; applied to men and beasts.. The term *cimarrón* is stated to be still applied in Cuba to fugitive slaves or outlawed negroes hidden in the woods or mountains. "Marooning" was a term which afterwards came to denote the infamous practice of leaving seamen behind on a desert island or "cay," as a punishment.

system of warfare; and in their frequent skirmishes with the troops sent out against them, acquired an art of attack and defence, which, in the difficult and hardly accessible fastnesses of the interior of the island, often foiled the utmost exertions of disciplined bravery.

At length, in the year 1733, the administration began to be weary of the ineffectual system so long pursued, by which Cudjoe's party had been greatly augmented. The island at this time had but few regular troops. Some regiments had been sent out from England, and sent back again; the fact being that such troops were not suited for the work required. To have called out the militia would have been injurious to the prosperity of the colony; it was, therefore, thought best that independent companies should be raised, to be commanded by officers chosen for their vigour, activity, and knowledge of the country; the militia being only occasionally called out to assist. A body of Indians from the Mosquito coast were also engaged, who proved of great service in the mountain warfare, and in tracing the haunts of the Maroons. Barracks and advanced fortified posts were also erected wherever deemed requisite.

Cudjoe, finding his haunts accessible to the

rangers who were stationed at the barracks, and the communication of his foraging parties in the back parts of Clarendon cut off, resolved to change his position, and to seek a situation of greater security. Accordingly, he established his headquarters at a district in the interior country, of most difficult access, called the Cockpits; a sort of valley, surrounded by precipices, and rocks, and mountains, in the caverns of which they secreted their women and children and deposited their ammunition. The choice was highly judicious, as in case of alarm he could throw himself into the Cockpit, whence no valour nor force could drive him; and the parishes of St James, Hanover, Westmoreland, and St. Elizabeth lay open to his predatory incursions, presenting more extensive and less defensible frontiers, and affording greater facilities for obtaining supplies from different quarters.

In this situation did these people maintain themselves, in a state of savage freedom, for eight or nine years, living in indolence while their provisions lasted, and ravaging the country when compelled by want. In their inroads they exercised the most horrible barbarities. Force after force had been in vain employed to subdue them; their hostile operations were carried on with unremitted daring. At length the colonists resolved to make every sacrifice, and use every exertion, to put an end to so harassing a war. All who could carry arms volunteered their services, and a large body was thus assembled under the command of Colonel Guthrie of the militia, and Captain Sadler of the regulars. It was deemed of the utmost importance that there should be no uncertainty in the prosecution of the most vigorous measures, the failure of which might operate most prejudicially on the minds of the slave population by convincing them of the power of the Maroons to maintain a successful opposition to the Government. The Governor, Edward Trelawney, was therefore urged by the principal persons of the country to offer terms of peace.

This being resolved upon, Guthrie and Sadler were directed to communicate the offers to Cudjoe as speedily as possible. They could not but be acceptable to the Maroons, who were equally tired of war. The formidable preparations made against them threw a great difficulty in the way of negotiation; for the Maroons could not reconcile these with the offers of peace, and the sincerity of the Government was doubted.

Governed by this motive, the wary Cudjoe collected his force, and waited the approach of the negotiators, on a spot the most favourable to action in his mode of warfare, where his people might defend themselves if treachery were intended. His men were posted on the ledges of rocks that rose almost perpendicularly to a great height on each side of a narrow defile. Guthrie, making the best disposition of his troops that the nature of the ground would admit of, marched on till he observed the smoke of their huts within a few hundred yards, when he called out in a loud tone that he was come by the Governor's order to make them an offer of terms and treat for peace, which the white people sincerely desired. An answer was returned that the Maroons wished the same, with the request that the troops might be kept back. In order to show the confidence he had in their sincerity, the Colonel proposed to them to send forward a person to assure them of his own.

This being readily assented to, a Dr. Russell was selected for this purpose, who, when he had approached near their huts, was met by two Maroons. After awhile the great negro leader consented to appear on the scene. He is described as a man short in stature, very stout, with strong African features, and a peculiar wildness in his manners. He had a hump on his back, partly covered by the tattered remains of an old blue coat; on his right side hung a cow's horn with powder, and a bag of large cut slugs; on the left he wore a machett, or *couteau*, in a leather sheath. At length, after some parleying, it was arranged that an unarmed deputation of a few gentlemen should come forward to witness the attestation of the mutual oath of peace. Cudjoe persuaded some of his people to descend from the rocks, not, however, without their arms. As the gentlemen approached, Guthrie advanced to him holding out his hand, which Cudjoe seized and kissed, and then, throwing himself upon the ground, embraced the Colonel's feet and asked his pardon. He seemed to have lost all his ferocity; and the rest of the Maroons, following his example, prostrated themselves, and expressed the most unbounded joy at the proceedings; and there was little less satisfaction experienced by the white men at the termination of the war. Cudjoe admitted that he had been for some time in a state of despondency and want.

There, under a large cotton-tree, the treaty was concluded in solemn terms, to the satisfaction of all parties. The negroes were weary of their way of life, and promised inviolable fidelity to the Government. They were declared free then and for ever; they were to administer their own laws in their community; to assist the Government whenever called upon; fifteen hundred acres between Trelawney Town and the Cockpits were to be granted them in perpetuity; and two officers nominated by the Governor were constantly to reside with them to maintain a friendly correspondence.

The submission of Cudjoe was quickly followed by that of Quao, and of the Windward rebels in the Portland district.

Thus was internal peace assured for the time—and for the first time—to the island. Cudjoe and his adherents faithfully maintained the conditions of the treaty.

The Maroons proved themselves a useful body as a rural police, not only in apprehending runaway slaves, for which their wild habits peculiarly adapted them, but also by supporting the regular forces in suppression of insurrection of the slaves, which every now and then broke out; they also came forward to assist when invasion appeared imminent.

To the honour of some of the negroes, they were in several instances first to give information of the murderous plots of the conspirators, and risked their lives amongst their fellows, in order to save the lives of their white masters, to whom they were attached.

The vast number of African slaves imported annually, representing tribes as diverse in character as different European nations, created a motley and dangerous population, amongst which the mysterious terrors of Obeism were employed in organizing plots with the greatest secrecy.

Amicable relations with the Maroons were, however, destined to come to an end, owing to what appears to have been culpable mismanagement on the part of the Government. In 1795 the Maroons of Trelawney brought under the notice of the Governor, the Earl of Balcarras, sundry matters of which they thought they had cause to complain. Inquiry into their grievances, with firmness and judicious conciliation, might have calmed the agitation, and at that period it was of vital importance to keep the island free from internal disaffection ; for the revolt of the negroes in St. Domingo, attended with diabolical atrocities, the breaking out of war between Great Britain and France, and the abolition of slavery in the French colonies, placed Jamaica in a new and fearful position. French refugees were constantly arriving in Jamaica, and the Governor seems to have entertained an opinion that the riotous conduct of the Maroons was instigated by French intrigues, although no grounds for that apprehension appear, and that the most stringent measures were required to arrest the contagion of French revolutionary principles.

The Government of Jamaica had petitioned the mother country for the protection of an additional military force, in consequence of the perilous aspect of affairs around them; and the Governor of Jamaica had received instructions to support legitimate authority, and to assist in the reduction of the rebels, by taking possession of such districts of St. Domingo as might solicit the protection of the British Empire. The 62nd and the 83rd Regiments, with detachments of the 18th and 20th Dragoons, were embarked in order to proceed to Hayti, when accounts of the turbulent behaviour of the Trelawney Maroons were received. The Governor therefore countermanded the men-of-war, and ordered that the troops should be disembarked in Montego Bay. The militia was called out, so that there was an available field force of about five thousand men, and the whole island was placed under martial law. The Maroons were informed that they were surrounded, and were summoned to surrender in three days on pain of death.

This defiant message had the effect of exasperating those independent people, who immediately set fire to their towns and fled to the woods and mountains. There they were unassailable; prices were set on their heads, £20 for a man, £10 for a woman, but none were brought in. The troops, on the contrary, were meeting with daily losses; whenever they approached the fastnesses, volleys with deadly effect were discharged at them by unseen hands, without any possibility of returning the fire—a handful of men, probably not more than five hundred capable of bearing arms, keeping at bay the whole British force.

So matters went on from August to December, when, in hopelessness of compelling submission by the usual modes of fighting, other auxiliaries were brought into the field, not unknown in the past history of the island. One hundred chasseurs and forty bloodhounds were imported from Cuba. This circumstance caused great public scandal; the idea of hunting human beings with dogs, and of renewing the cruelties formerly perpetrated by the Spaniards, was pronounced horrible, and imagination painted bleeding corpses mangled by their ferocious pursuers. However, no injury of this sort occurred. Dallas gives this highly interesting description of them. "On coming up with a fugitive," he says, "they bark at him till he stops; they then crouch near him, terrifying him with a ferocious growling if he stirs. In this position they continue barking, to give notice to the chasseurs, who come up and secure their prisoner." *

The arrival of these "dogs of war" had its desired effect. The bloodhounds did not seize the Maroons, but terror did, and they shortly afterwards surrendered. General Walpole appears to have conducted the military operations with as much humanity as possible, and he endeavoured from the first to make terms with them. On the 1st of January, 1796, he ratified a treaty with them on these terms :—

That they should ask pardon ; that they should proceed to such place as should be appointed ; and that they should deliver up all runaways.

A joint committee of the Council and Assembly was appointed to consider the best way of disposing of the prisoners, and it was resolved to transport them to Nova Scotia. General Walpole protested against this act, and when rewards were liberally voted to all concerned, he declined to accept the proffered grant of five hundred guineas for the purchase of a sword of honour. He soon after left the island, and retired from the army.

Mr. Bryan Edwards, who had returned from Jamaica, and had just been elected member for the borough of Grampound in Cornwall, in his place in

* "History of the Maroons," ii.

Parliament, offered the following explanation of the cause of the outbreak:*—"Two Maroons having been found guilty of felony in the town of Montego Bay, were tried according to law, and according to the very letter of the treaty, and sentenced to receive a few lashes at a cart's tail. The sentence was mild, and the punishment not severe, but the whole body of the Trelawney Town Maroons, in revenge for the indignity offered to two of their number, immediately took up arms, and soon afterwards actually proceeded to set fire to the plantations. The gallant officer (General Walpole) had undoubtedly the merit, under the judicious orders of the Earl of Balcarras, of putting an end to the most unnatural and unprovoked rebellion; and if those two distinguished persons differed in opinion concerning the terms on which the Maroons surrendered, it is much to be lamented. The Maroons," he added, "did not comply with the conditions; they did not surrender on the day fixed, and they did not give up the fugitive negroes." He urged that the Assembly considered that men who had violated their allegiance, and entered into a bloody and cruel war without provocation, were unfit to remain in the island; yet, in the disposal of these

* *Ann. Reg.*, xxxix. 129.

people, a degree of generosity and tenderness had been manifested which is without example. After providing them with fit and proper clothing for a change of climate, the Assembly sent three gentlemen with them to America, with a sum of £25,000, to purchase lands for their future maintenance. Mr. Edwards, in reply to some observations of Mr. Wilberforce, stated that to his certain knowledge the Maroons were cannibals.

"It is not easy to say," writes Gardner (p. 236), "what this wretched affair really cost. In April, 1796, £372,000 was stated in the Assembly as the amount then known. Other bills came in afterwards, and by the end of the year it was found that from a comparatively small amount the island's debt had risen to nearly half a million."

The subsequent history of the Trelawney Maroons is soon told: £47,000 was expended in providing for their wants for three years after their arrival in Nova Scotia, the climate of which was ill adapted to a West Indian constitution. They were then removed to Sierra Leone, where lands were assigned to them, on which they settled quietly, and their descendants are now among the most respectable of the negro settlers in Free Town and its neighbourhood.*

* Gardner, 238.

The Accompong Maroons remained faithful to their allegiance. Even in the great outbreak of the slaves in 1831, caused by the emancipation debates in England, the attempts to incite them to join the rebellion entirely failed. Maroons and Maroon towns still exist in Jamaica, and they are still a privileged class; but their special avocations have almost ceased. The pursuit of wild boars has terminated with the rewards for fugitive slaves, and importations of American bacon have driven out of the market the "jerked hog" of the Maroon.

In 1754 an Act was passed to divide the island into three counties, namely, Cornwall, Middlesex, and Surrey. In the same year Admiral Knowles, the Governor, removed the seat of government from Spanish Town to Kingston, and the public records were then brought from the former to the latter. At that time Spanish Town had no building suited for the residence of a governor, or convenient for legislative purposes. The legislators seem not to have been very punctilious in the selection of their place of meeting. When the Supreme Court was in session at Spanish Town, it often assembled in the parish church, and committees were convened in taverns, coffee-houses, and even at private residences.* This measure,

* Gardner, 107.

although disapproved of only by two members of the Legislative Council, was warmly opposed, and many petitions against it were sent to the home Government. It was not sanctioned, and in October, 1758, Moore, the succeeding Governor, issued the royal command which restored Spanish Town to metropolitan dignity. Thirty waggons, laden with the records, and escorted by a party of foot soldiers, left Kingston at 1 A.M., and, having been met by a detachment of the troops quartered in Spanish Town, arrived there about 9 A.M., amidst the acclamations of the people. A grand entertainment was given, an ox was roasted, and the town illuminated.*

To secure their town as far as possible against any future attempts to deprive it of its privileges, the public buildings were commenced around the central square, comprising a residence for the Governor, a senate-house, assize-courts, and other state requirements. Thirty years elapsed before all were completed. King's House, as it is still called, was completed in 1763, at a cost of £18,000 according to Gardner (p. 136), £30,000 according to Bridges (ii. 103), and £50,000 according to Philippo.†

* Ann. Reg., ii. 57.
† "Jamaica, Past and Present," 1843, p. 64.

In 1763 Fort Augusta, the large military establishment which occupied a promontory at the entrance to Kingston Harbour, opposite to Port Royal, was struck by lightning and destroyed by the explosion of its magazine, and a great amount of loss of life and property occurred in consequence.

The year 1782 beheld Great Britain at war with America, with France, Spain, and Holland. Amidst external dangers to the island, a conflagration, at one time threatening the total destruction of Kingston, burst forth. The wind providentially changed, and the remainder of the town was saved, but not before property estimated at nearly a million sterling was consumed by the devouring element. From greater evils still—the horrors of war and famine—Jamaica was spared by one of the most brilliant achievements of modern history. The victory over the French fleet on the 12th of April, preventing the junction of the French and Spanish fleets, saved the island from inevitable invasion and conquest by an overwhelming force. Rodney gained a deserved peerage; and a marble statue, executed by Bacon at a cost of 3,000 guineas, was erected to his honour in the square at Spanish Town, since removed, amidst the protests of the inhabitants, to Kingston.

CHAPTER XII.

JAMAICA (*continued*).

THE Government of Jamaica was framed after the model of that of the parent state. It consisted of a Governor, appointed by the Crown; a Council similar to the Privy Council of England, or to the House of Lords, without its independence, being appointed by the Crown at the recommendation of the Governor; and an Assembly, or House of Representatives, chosen by a small portion of the people, and enjoying all the privileges of the English House of Commons. The executive virtually resided in the Governor, and his acts, even if contrary to the Council, were held valid. The Council, with the Governor, constituted a Court of Error and Appeal from the Common Law Courts. In the event of the death or absence of the Governor or Lieutenant-Governor, the eldest member of the Council assumed the government with the title of President of the island.

The House of Assembly ultimately consisted of forty-five members, being two representatives for each parish, and an additional one for Spanish Town, Kingston, and Port Royal. The Septennial Act was in force here, and the qualification was a freehold of £300 per annum, or a real and personal estate of £3,000. It was required that an elector should possess, in the parish in which he was registered, a freehold estate of the value of £6, or a rent-charge of £30, that he should be twenty-one years of age, pay taxes to the amount of £3 per annum, and produce a certificate that his taxes had been paid.

But though the legislature enacted its own laws, those laws were subject to their confirmation or rejection by the sovereign in council; others of a more special and important character were passed with a suspensory clause, and were not carried into effect until the sovereign's pleasure had been made known. The Crown had the prerogative of refusing assent to any colonial act which had not been previously confirmed at any period, however remote. Although the common law of England was, and is, here in force, it was not so generally with statute law. To some colonial enactments the statute law of England would be inapplicable. The "Consolidated Slave

Act," for instance, existed as a distinct code, having reference to slavery and its relations alone.

Each parish, comprising a very large territorial district, has a civil officer, styled a "Custos," answering to a lord-lieutenant of a county in England; he is designated "Honourable," and has the custody of the parochial records.

The anti-slavery debates in the British Houses of Parliament were not without their effect in the colonies. The slaves could not be unconcerned listeners to the discussions at their masters' tables. The consequence was that great excitement prevailed among them; it grew rapidly, and ultimately ripened, in 1831, into the most dangerous rebellion the island had ever yet witnessed, and the missionaries (especially the Baptists) were charged by the planters with having fomented it. It arose from a misapprehension in the minds of the negro population that orders had come out from England for their immediate emancipation. The slaves in Jamaica have never given any indication of ability for extended organization; at that time there was a general understanding among them but no combined movement—a providential circumstance, for, according to published returns, there were at this time 307,254 slaves in the island.* There were still found on this as on former occasions a faithful few, who defended their masters' lives and property against their fellow-negroes.

The Government was alive to the danger; martial law was proclaimed, and Sir Willoughby Cotton, as commander-in-chief, at the head of a large force, was invested by the Governor, the Earl of Belmore, with all the authority he could confer. English soldiers and local militia scoured the country in all directions. The rebels, being in small scattered parties, whenever the troops encountered them were invariably defeated. On many of the estates the negroes refused to work, and on the appearance of the military fled into the woods. Such a state of things might have continued for an indefinite period, but a short soldierly address of the General produced a wonderful effect. He assured them that the report of the King having made them free was devoid of foundation, that resistance was folly, and that, though rebels deserved death, yet, if they would surrender, mercy should be shown to all except the ringleaders and incendiaries. In the ensuing month of February the Governor visited Montego Bay; he there found 363 prisoners in the jail.

* Gardner, 269.

Ninety-four reputed rebels had been hanged in that town alone, and frequently eighteen or twenty flogged in a single day. Ascertaining that there was a great inclination for a general surrender if kind treatment could be secured, he issued a proclamation offering a pardon to all (except specified individuals) who should surrender within ten days, and two days after he declared martial law to be at an end; and thus this rebellion, the aspect of which had been so formidable, was at an end.

Now came the cry of discontent from the whites, and the wail of those who were not satiated with retaliation. These complained that all clemency shown to the negroes served only to instigate them to further insubordination. The object of many of the planters evidently was to use the late deplorable events as arguments against emancipation, and as reasons for binding still more firmly the shackles of slavery. The request of the British Secretary for the Colonies, that the legislature of Jamaica would reconsider the dispatches transmitted in 1823, having reference to the amelioration of the condition of the slaves with a view to their gradual emancipation, was treated with general contempt. Inflammatory speeches were made throughout the island, both in public and private, against the missionaries and the British Government, accompanied by menaces of rebellion on the part of the white inhabitants against the parent state, and a transfer of their allegiance to some more natural mother. Much foolish bluster was written and spoken. A local newspaper reminded its readers that "the slaves were not his Majesty's subjects, but the property of their owners, confirmed by laws which his Majesty's ancestors had recognised, and which were then in force."* A member of the House of Assembly talked wildly of physical force and the ability of the militia to resist the forces of the mother country! † The more moderate admitted the supremacy of the sovereign, but not that of a portion of his Majesty's subjects at home over another portion of those subjects in Jamaica. In the meanwhile chapels were burned down, and missionaries went about in danger of their lives. Who were the rebels then? Yet martial law was not proclaimed.

In the judgment of the people of Great Britain slaves were his Majesty's subjects, and the time had arrived when they must be brought under legislation. The calm dignity of the Imperial

* *Jamaica Courant*, June 18, 1834.
† Gardner, p. 284.

Parliament was undisturbed by the petulance of the colonists, and the grandest and most merciful Act that ever passed through any house of legislature was introduced by the Colonial Secretary, Mr. Stanley, on the 20th of May, 1833. He stated that it was not without extreme reluctance that his Majesty's Government had taken upon itself the responsibility of recommending to the Imperial Parliament the exercise of their undoubted right to interpose paramount authority in legislating for the internal regulation of the colonies; but all attempts to induce the slave-owners to deal with the matter having failed, the British nation, through its representatives, was now called on to suppress the evil of slavery. He then proposed a series of resolutions providing for gradual abolition. Children born after the passing of the Act, and all those under six years of age, were declared free. Others were to be registered as apprentices, and to work for their former owners for six years if field labourers, or four years if domestic servants.

As it was felt, however, that the planters ought not to suffer exclusively by emancipation, for slavery had been recognised and fostered by English laws, a proposed loan of fifteen millions was changed into a gift of twenty, of which rather more than six were appropriated to Jamaica.

The apprenticeship scheme was found not to answer after an experience of four years. On May 22nd, 1838, Parliament resolved, "that negro apprenticeship in the British colonies should at once cease and determine," which Alison records as "the hazardous step, which has completed the ruin of the West Indies."* The Earl of Mulgrave (afterwards Marquis of Normanby) having succeeded to the government of Jamaica, by a happy combination of wisdom, firmness, and energy, had restored tranquillity to the distracted community, and induced the House of Assembly to accede to the proposals of the parent state. His task was one requiring great delicacy and judgment, as he had to enforce laws held in detestation by the great mass of proprietors, who predicted ruin and bloodshed as the inevitable consequence of emancipation. Lieutenant-General Sir Lionel Smith was the Governor when emancipation was proclaimed and celebrated with the greatest rejoicings, unmarred by any of those disasters which had been prognosticated. What effect free labour has had in the great diminution of the exports of the colony is not a matter to be discussed here.

The year 1838 found the House of Assembly in collision with the home Government. Parliament

* "History of Europe," v. 430.

had passed a bill to provide for the better government of jails in the West Indies, and this act was considered an infringement on colonial rights. Is it not questionable if it were not so? After the expression of the extreme reluctance with which his Majesty's Government had recommended the interposition of the Imperial Parliament in legislating for the internal regulation of the chartered colonies, which was the minister's preface in introducing so wide a question as the emancipation of all the slaves in the dominions of Great Britain, it does seem that it was an usurpation of power, and an infringement of the inherent rights of the legislature of Jamaica, to enforce the adoption of a system of prison discipline. The House of Assembly was still smarting under the infliction of the late amended Abolition Act, and "the members now resolved that they would abstain from all exercise of legislative functions, except such as might be necessary to preserve inviolate the faith of the island with the public creditor, until it was known if they were to be treated as subjects having the power of making laws, or to be governed by the British Parliament and by orders in council." *

The House of Assembly was thereupon dis-

* Gardner, p. 401.

solved by the Governor. A new one was convened, which immediately resolved "to adhere to the resolutions which the late House had agreed, which had been fully sanctioned by the constituency of the island." This declaration was fatal to the existence of this House, and it was summarily dissolved.

When the British Government became acquainted with the state of affairs, it was felt that the rebellious legislature must be coerced into submission; and it was determined to introduce a measure into Parliament suspending the constitution of the island for a term of five years, during which period a provisional Government, consisting of the Governor and Council, was to administer its affairs.

On the 9th April, 1839, Mr. Labouchere, then Under-Secretary of State for the Colonies, brought forward the proposed measure. It was carried, after a long debate, in a full house, by a majority of only five. This was tantamount to a defeat, and the ministers announced their resignation. Sir Robert Peel was called upon to form a cabinet, a work in which he met with unexpected difficulties in consequence of the questions which arose in relation to the appointments of the ladies of her Majesty's household.

The result was the return of Lord Melbourne to office. A new Jamaica bill was introduced and passed. It allowed the Assembly time to re-enact those annual laws which were positively necessary to the credit and good order of the island, but should it refuse, the Governor in Council was empowered to pass them at the expiration of two months.*

Sir Charles Metcalfe (afterwards raised to the peerage for his services), an Indian statesman of deserved celebrity, was selected as a fitting person to guide the destinies of the island at this trying time. In his opening address to the House of Assembly on the 22nd October, 1839, he expressed an anxious hope that past differences might be buried in oblivion, and that there would be no occasion to call into exercise the recent act of the Imperial Legislature, elicited by the late contest. He was there, he said, to preserve inviolable their laws and constitution, subject to those laws by which the whole empire was governed. Peculiar circumstances had necessitated a considerable amount of legislation for the colonies at large; but the great measure of emancipation having been completed, there was no reason to anticipate further interference with

* Hansard, vol. xlvii. p. 1119.

the action of local legislatures, unless it was of a tendency to counteract or retard the benefits designed by that measure.*

This declaration was received with a general burst of applause, and in reply the House asserted that it had contended only for the free exercise of deliberate judgment in enacting its laws, and had never claimed a right to pass any inconsistent with the general interests of the kingdom.

The struggle was at an end. The professions which the Governor made at the opening were fully borne out to the close of his short administration. The greatest harmony characterized the proceedings of every branch of the legislature; and when ill-health compelled his resignation in 1842, he carried with him the gratitude of the community, which was perpetuated by the naming of a new parish after him, and by the vote of 3,000 guineas for a statue, now erected in Central Park, Kingston. †

In the altered circumstances of the times, the House of Assembly, if not always, was certainly now, a barrier in the way of all progress. It was the mouthpiece of the planters, but could

---

* Kay's "Life of Lord Metcalfe," i. 388.

† The statue is of granite, nine feet high, designed by Baily.

scarcely be regarded as a representative body; for with a population of over half a million, the united registries in 1864 showed only 1,903 persons qualified to vote, and at the last general election, held that year, only 1,457 persons exercised their privilege. The highest number of votes recorded for any one candidate was in Kingston, where 303 were given for Mr. Jordon; thirty-two members elected had less than fifty votes each; and twenty-five of these had less than thirty. With constituencies so small it was easy for any man to obtain a seat; and there was no representation of the great body of the people, for whom the Assembly professed to legislate. In the county of Cornwall, containing five large parishes, and a third of the entire population of the island, there were only 246 voters, 162 of whom returned ten members.*

For the past thirty years the character of the House had been gradually deteriorating; and its deliberations were often interrupted by scenes of confusion and strife. The violent language so often used in the House was not without influence on the people at large. At public meetings expressions of a very seditious character were commonly employed, and a turbulent spirit exhi-

* Appendix, Blue Book, 1863.

bited itself in many parts of the island. The community had grave reasons for complaint; for, while the Assembly was wasting time in wrangling about its so-called privileges and rights, glaring abuses in almost all public institutions remained unredressed, and very little was done to promote the social elevation or true prosperity of the country. It was under such circumstances that the fearful outbreak occurred under Governor Eyre, promoted for the first time in the annals of negro rebellion in Jamaica by a man of superior intelligence to their race.*

During slavery the negroes were maintained principally by the produce of their own provision grounds, allotted to them for that purpose on the estates, and which they cultivated in the time allowed them by their masters for that purpose. When emancipated, being constitutionally indisposed to anything like regular labour, they avoided it as much as possible, and squatted upon the land, the produce of which would, with hardly any exertion, afford them sustenance. This disposition was unhappily encouraged to

---

* G. W. Gordon, son of Joseph Gordon, a great planting attorney; his mother was a woman of colour. He had a mania for the acquisition of land, but it never paid under his management, and at the time of his death it was all mortgaged. His admitted liabilities amounted to £35,000.—Gardner, 475.

the utmost by their professed friends—philanthropists some of them—who ever since emancipation had done their utmost to inspire them with an aversion to labour, and a notion that they were entitled to have land rent free, or, at all events, that labour was not to be enforced by making it a condition of the possession of land. "Either work on our estates or pay rent," was the planters' proposal; but the negroes wanted to enjoy the produce-lands rent free, as they had enjoyed them in slavery, and also to be free to work or not, as they pleased, and where it suited them.

The benevolent Quaker, Joseph J. Gurney, who visited the island in 1840, wrote, "The peasantry of Jamaica are much too cognizant of their own rights and interests long to submit to this new form of slavery." *

It must be manifest that, with a population so impulsive and excitable, the constant exercise of influences of this kind must have a perpetual tendency to create insurrection.

Earl Grey expressed himself that "the measure for the abolition of slavery was generally admitted to have been unhappily defective, from its containing no provisions calculated to meet

* "Six Months in the West Indies," p. 102.

the altered state of society, and the want of adequate motive for labour," and "that in consequence the negro had become addicted to idleness and vice, and that the rising generation were more disposed to lawless and reckless courses than their elders." *

External events were favourable to the development of the Liberation sentiment. The emancipation of the black race in North America consequent upon the war between the Northern and Southern States, a revolution in Hayti then going on,† were circumstances combining to render any insurrection terribly perilous. It must be remembered that Jamaica is only one day's sail from Hayti or St. Domingo, where the horrors of negro insurrection had been again and again realised, and where by the preponderance of numbers the blacks had achieved not only emancipation but independence by the ruthless perpetration of repeated massacres, and had established a negro state, which has ever since been a standing temptation to the blacks in Jamaica and a standing

* "Colonial Policy," i. 59.
† The capture of a schooner under English colours at Port Antonio on October 25, 1865, with General Lamothe and five other Haytians on board, and one hundred kegs of gunpowder, was considered confirmatory of the suspicions of complicity.—"Minutes of Evidence, Royal Commission," p. 997.

menace to the white population. At the last census, in 1871, there were 392,707 blacks and 13,101 whites. In St. Domingo the negroes were nearly half a million, but the whites in much greater proportion. The case of Jamaica was one therefore of far greater peril.*

Anticipations of negro insurrection were at a somewhat later period signally verified by the rebellion which broke out during the governorship of Mr. Eyre. Gordon, the leading instigator, and others had been traversing the island, inciting the people to disaffection. He told them (in August, 1865) that they "must do what Hayti does." † The extermination of the whites was an avowed sentiment. ." Buckra country for us,"—"Neber mind Buckra women, we can get them when we want,"—"Colour for Colour," —"We want blood,"—such were the expressions indicating the prevailing feeling. Incendiary fires were few, but that was explained by the remarks, "Don't burn the trash-house, we want sugar to make for ourselves,"—"Don't set fire to the house, only kill the white man, we have the house to live in ourselves." ‡

---

* "Considerations on the case of Mr. Eyre," by W. F. Finlaison.
† "Minutes," p. 444.
‡ "Report of Jamaica Royal Commission," p. 16.

For some months previous to the outbreak meetings had been held, at which oaths were administered and names of confederates recorded. Bodies of men had been drilled in different places with a degree of organization, several persons being named as colonels and captains.* Rendered bold by numbers, the negro population was ready to break out into open rebellion, had not the prompt measures of the Governor arrested the calamity. "It might have been well," says Gardner,† "if, when so many revolutionary sentiments were being expressed or printed, active measures had been taken to arrest the mischief by prosecuting some of the ringleaders; but it was generally understood that the Attorney-General was opposed to such a course, under the impression that it would make these persons more important by constituting them, in the estimation of their friends, political martyrs."

This may have been the general understanding. Governor Eyre does not say so in his evidence, but clearly "it was no secret that there were persons who declared their intention of going from parish to parish, telling the people that they were oppressed."

A collision with the police in a trifling case of

* "Report of Jamaica Royal Commission," p. 13.
† "History of Jamaica," p. 474.

assault at Morant Bay, on Saturday, October 7, 1865, precipitated matters, and produced the first resistance to lawful authority. On the Wednesday following, a crowd of men, armed with cutlasses, sticks, and a few muskets and bayonets plundered from the police-station, threw themselves upon the magistracy, the police, and the volunteers. The court-house, where the authorities had taken refuge, was set on fire, and most of the inmates who were driven out by the flames were brutally murdered or maltreated: eighteen, including the Custos, were killed, and about thirty-one severely wounded. After this the town remained in possession of the rioters. The gaolers were compelled to throw open the prison doors, and fifty-one prisoners were released.

Next day, Bath, eight miles to the north-east of Morant Bay, was visited by an armed party with flags flying and drums beating, which held complete possession of the town till the following day, when, on hearing the well-known horn of the Maroons, who, at the request of a magistrate resident there, came to the relief of the inhabitants, the rioters fled with precipitation. The stores in the town were pillaged, and property to a large amount was carried off or destroyed. The few white and almost all the coloured inhabitants fled to the bush. Several estates in the neighbourhood were attacked in the course of that day and night: at one of these a body of fifty men variously armed, under the command of a person addressed as Captain Wilson, killed the bookkeeper, and the life of the owner's son was saved only through the intercession of his coloured overseer.

At Amity Hall a mob of four hundred men murdered the owner, and his son was left for dead; a stipendiary magistrate and another gentleman were severely wounded.

Many attempts had been made by the insurgent leaders, before the breaking out and during the progress of the rebellion, to obtain the co-operation of the Maroons.

But this singular and interesting people—occupying as they do a mountainous district, difficult of access, and commanding the road from the north to the south of the island, so that they could have afforded most valuable assistance to any rising which might take place in St. Thomas-in-the-East—remained unswerving in their loyalty, and gave every possible assistance in suppressing the rebellion.* Amid this murderous treachery it is a relief to note the many instances of noble

* "Report," p. 14.

devotion on the part of black servants, and their efforts to save the lives and property of their masters, which may be found interspersed in the "Minutes of Evidence."*

In consequence of the disturbed state of the districts of St. George's-in-the-East, the Custos, Baron Ketelhodt, had written to the Governor, on the 10th October, requesting military aid. The letter was received by him at Spanish Town next morning. Expresses were immediately sent off to Major-General O'Connor at Kingston, requesting him to get ready 100 men for immediate embarkation; and to the senior naval officer at Port Royal, with the request that a man-of-war might convey them at once to Morant Bay. They reached their destination next day, but only in time to preserve that place from a second attack by the insurgents. On the morning of the 12th the Governor received information of the events of the 11th, and also that a body of the insurgents was marching up the valley on the line of the Yallahs River. An additional force was, in consequence, sent off without delay to Morant Bay.

The Privy Council was then summoned, and came unanimously to the conclusion that it was essential at once to proclaim martial law. By a

* "Minutes," p. 920, and elsewhere; also "Report," p. 15.

recent Act of the Jamaica legislature (9 Vict. c. 35) it was provided that martial law should not be proclaimed in future except by the consent of a council of war, to be composed of the Governor, the Privy Council, members of the House of Assembly, with certain naval and military officers; not less than twenty-one being required as a quorum.

This council met on the morning of the 13th, attended by about thirty members, among whom were men of all parties in the island. It was unanimously resolved that martial law should be at once declared over the whole of the county of Surrey with the exception of the town of Kingston.

The Royal Commissioners in their Report express their opinion that "the council of war had good reason for the advice which they gave, and that the Governor was well justified in acting upon that advice," and that the "military arrangements were prompt and judicious," and "by confining the insurgents to the parish of St. Thomas-in-the-East and its neighbourhood, the disturbances were kept in check, and were prevented from spreading to other parts of the island" (pp. 19, 20).

Detachments composed of the West India regiments serving in Jamaica were dispatched to Morant Bay and to Port Antonio, and a party of the 2nd Battalion 6th Regiment marched from Newcastle along the line of the Blue Mountain Valley to intercept the insurgents, who were reported to be advancing by that route.

Bodies of Maroons protected Port Antonio and Bath. Blue-jackets and marines were also landed at Morant Bay from H.M.S. *Wolverine* to co-operate with the regular troops, and the man-of-war in returning brought away refugees, so that Kingston became crowded with them. One detachment of the 6th Regiment marched down south from Newcastle to Gordon Town, and another proceeded north to Annotto Bay, so that the county of Surrey was completely hemmed in. The Governor was justified in believing that he had to put down not a mere casual insurrection, but a formidable rebellion—a concerted rising with a general object, certain to spread owing to community of feeling and sympathies of race. It was, therefore, a matter of absolute necessity and self-defence to make an example, which, by striking terror, might deter other districts from following the example of St. Thomas-in-the-East. The evidence before the Commissioners proves the excited state of various districts in the island; and that had the rebellion in the east not been so summarily suppressed, the black population throughout the island would have been in revolt, the result of which would have been an universal massacre, for the military force was numerically far too weak to offer a successful resistance.

A witness of consideration stated that the danger during this outbreak was far greater than in that of the year 1831; for at that time there were five white regiments in the island, 9,100 well-trained militia, 540 horsemen, and about 14,000 Maroons.* In 1865 there were 1,000 soldiers to control the enormous black population, and to protect the few thousands of white people scattered everywhere throughout a country intersected by chains of mountains, by woods, by rivers, and ravines, always difficult of access, and in the rainy season, which it then was, almost impassable. The greatest terror naturally pervaded the inhabitants of the better class. The white population of the entire parish of St. Thomas-in-the-East, according to the census of 1861, was only 282 persons, women and children included, and the black amounted to 23,230. That many of these were on the side of law and order is unquestionable; but the fear of massacre was great, and till the troops arrived the insurgents did whatever they desired.

The total strength of the regular forces employed

* "Minutes," p. 926.

in the actual suppression of the rebellion was only 472 of all arms and ranks, viz. :—*

Royal Artillery	20
2nd Battalion 6th Royal Regiment	71
1st West India Regiment	199
Late 5th West India Regiment, volunteers to other corps	56
Naval Brigade, officers, seamen, and marines	126
	472
The number of Maroons employed was	287

After the detachment had been dispatched to the north from Newcastle, there remained only about 300 men to guard the military station and to supply any further demands for troops. In consequence of apprehended disturbances at Linstead, in the parish of St. Thomas-in-the-Vale, about fourteen miles to the north-west of Spanish Town, the troops from that place were sent thither, leaving the seat of government denuded of troops for the time being. Volunteers, pensioners, and special constables were enrolled for the protection of Kingston and for the general maintenance of order. On the 28th October 200 men arrived in the W. I. and Pacific Company's steamer *Plantagenet* from Nassau, and on the next day H.M.S. *Urgent* brought 533 from Barbadoes.†

* "Minutes," p. 1114.
† Royal Artillery, 48; 3rd (Buffs), 158; 2nd West India Regiment, 327.—"Minutes," p. 1001.

The details of the operations, as recorded in the dispatches and evidence in the Blue Book, are highly curious and interesting. A great mass of the evidence of uneducated negroes must, however, be utterly discredited. That the prompt measures taken were the means of preventing a general massacre, and of restoring peace and order, is unquestionable; but the maintenance of martial law, with its attendant severities, when the insurrection was, if not at an end, no longer dangerous, was not justifiable. Mr. Disraeli put the matter on the right footing when he said the justification depended on the nature of the emergency, and upon the question whether the measures taken were disproportioned to the emergency.

The total number of executions during the suppression amounted to 439.* Of these 147 persons were put to death after the 25th of October. Five days later an amnesty was declared, and the Governor certified that the Rebellion "*lately existing*" had been put down, yet martial law was continued until the 13th of November.† The sentences were in some cases carried into effect with an aggravation of cruelty. One is sorry to find recorded of gallant defenders such passages as these:—

* "Minutes," p. 1143. † Ibid., p. 87.

"I adopted a plan which has struck *immense* terror into these wretched men, far more than death; which is, I caused them to hang each other. They entreat to be shot to avoid this, which appears to me by far more dreadful an ordeal to them than death; and stranger still, they howl and shriek from a few lashes from a cat, whilst they calmly bow and remain unmoved at being shot."* Another officer writes: "H—— is doing splendid service with his men, shooting every black man who cannot account for himself (sixty on line of march). N—— hanging like fun, by court-martial." †

A reputed Obeah man was tried by court-martial, and convicted of being a rebel and attempting to poison. It was probably an example necessary to disabuse the minds of the negroes of the invulnerability of these people. "Buckra can't hurt dem," is a popular assertion and belief. So he was placed in a conspicuous position on a hill-side, about four hundred yards from the firing party. His death was instantaneous. It is stated that the effect on the minds of the prisoners was so great, that the commanding officer felt justified in releasing a considerable number of them. ‡

* "Minutes," p. 1122.   † Ibid., p. 1120.   ‡ Ibid., p. 762.

About 600 persons were flogged (at Bath, fifty in one day), twenty of whom, *horresco referens*, were women. Fifty and a hundred lashes were a frequent infliction.

An officer reports as his firm conviction, "Forty lashes have far more terror for them than death. The writhing and intense agony of the lash is frightful to witness, whereas being shot or hanged produces no more impression in them apparently than being let go." *

The total number of dwellings set on fire by the troops amounted to a thousand.

Great allowance must be made for the unusual and trying circumstances in which the troops were suddenly called upon to act so responsible a part. With a few exceptions they behaved admirably; their physical powers were tested to the utmost by long marches performed alternately under the blazing sun and the rains of the tropics.

Having repeatedly to cross rivers swollen to a perilous depth, and to proceed over marshy ground which destroyed their boots; they became blistered and foot-sore. Not a casualty occurred: not a single man fell out from the line of march: but after reading the evidence, it is impossible to

* "Minutes," p. 1122.

arrive at any other conclusion than that contained in the summary of the Report of the Royal Commissioners, that—

"The punishment of death was unnecessarily frequent.

"The floggings were reckless, and at Bath positively barbarous; and

"The burning of 1,000 houses was wanton and cruel."

While martial law was still in operation, the Assembly was convened. The Governor, after eulogising the conduct of those who had been engaged in the suppression of the outbreak, and enlarging upon the danger to which the island had been and was still exposed, stated that the want of the colony was a strong government; and to obtain it, he was of opinion there was but one course open, and that was that the existing form of constitution should be abolished, and another one substituted, "in which union, co-operation, consistency, and promptness of action might as far as possible be secured."[*]

The common peril had wrought wonderful unanimity—an agreement even in a suicidal proceeding. The address of the Council re-echoed

[* Gardner, p. 492.]

the sentiments of Governor Eyre; so also did that of the Assembly, which went so far as to assert that a strong government was necessary to save Jamaica from sinking "into the condition of a second Hayti."* A bill was forthwith introduced to alter the constitution; after some failures, on the 14th of December, an Act was passed, placing the future constitution entirely in the hands of the Imperial Government.

The special commissioners appointed to inquire into the origin and circumstances of the outbreak opened their court on the 20th of January, 1866, and their admirable conduct of the affair has elicited universal commendation. As a proof of the difficulty of their task, it may be stated that they examined 730 witnesses, which occupied fifty-one days. The President—the valuable public servant so lately deceased—Sir Henry Storks, was also empowered to act as Governor and Commander-in-chief during the course of the inquiry, and until the final decision of the British Government should be made known. On the 18th of June Mr. Cardwell, the Colonial Secretary, forwarded a dispatch in reply to the Report, in which it was stated that her Majesty's

* Gardner, p. 496.

Government, while giving Mr. Eyre full credit for some portions of his conduct, felt compelled to disapprove other portions. Mr. Eyre was in consequence not restored to the government, and so Sir Henry Storks continued in power. He again called the legislature together on the 6th January, 1866, but only to pass two bills necessary to carry out the purposes of the Royal Commission; and on the 10th of January the history of representative institutions in Jamaica terminated, after having existed for two hundred and two years.

Effect had been given by the Imperial Parliament to the enactment made by the Assembly to alter and amend the constitution, and the 29th and 30th Vict. c. 12 enacted "that the Council and House of Assembly should cease and determine absolutely, and in place of the legislature abolished it should be lawful for Her Majesty to create and constitute a government for that island in such form and with such powers as to her Majesty may best seem fitting."

The entire authority is now practically vested in the Governor, assisted by a Privy Council consisting of eight members, and a Legislative Council of six official and six non-official members, whose proceedings present a marked contrast to the angry debates and the class legislation of former days.

In August, 1866, Sir John Peter Grant, a distinguished Indian civilian, arrived as Govenor, and under his administration the condition of the island has steadily but visibly improved.

The Blue Book for 1874 contains the following satisfactory announcement: "The year 1871—72 is the fourth consecutive year in which a large surplus of revenue over expenditure has been obtained" (p. 32). Several changes have been effected under the new constitution; the most important have been the introduction, in 1868, of a system of popular education (the schools of every religious denomination being brought under government inspection),* and the disestablishment of the Church of England in 1870.

A local newspaper, the *Baptist Reporter*, gives the following summary of the religious census of Jamaica for 1871. I have no means of testing its accuracy, but one would guess that such items as "heathens and persons of no religion," "unknown," and "religion unreported," are introduced in order to make up the sum total of the population.

* The allowance for public instruction, which was only £4,622 in 1866, has now been raised to £19,403.—Blue Book.

Baptists	112,604
Bhuddists	75
Bible Christians and Plymouth Brethren	447
Christians (sect not given)	27,463
Congregationalists, London and American Mission	1,109
Episcopalians	184,263
Hindus	3,245
Jamaica Wesleyan Association	1,688
Jews	1,798
Mahommedans	1,137
Methodists (sect not given)	433
Moravians	18,032
Parsees	10
Presbyterians	18,033
United or Free Church	88
Primitive Christians	176
Protestants (sect not known)	17,814
Roman Catholics	9,483
Swedenborgians and Unitarians	15
Wesleyans	65,353
Heathens and persons of no religion	5,980
Lutherans	31
Unknown	252
Religion unreported	34,580
	506,154

In 1872, the seat of government was again transferred from Spanish Town to Kingston. The latter is unquestionably the most considerable place in the island, although the situation may not be the most generally convenient. An official residence for the Governor, formerly the Bishop's palace, was purchased near to Kingston, and the fine range of government buildings at Spanish

Town has been converted into an educational college.

The immigration of Coolies has proved a source of vast benefit to the colony, and has remedied to a great extent the evil arising from the indisposition to labour of the native black population. There are now about 11,000 Coolies in the island, who by their steady and industrious habits give entire satisfaction to their employers; and as a proof that these people are contented with their position, out of a number of 1,599 who in the year 1873 completed their term of service, only 420 elected to return to India. Thus almost three-fourths of the number entitled to a free passage home became free settlers in Jamaica. These 420 returning Coolies took with them £3,855 in Treasury bills, besides valuables and specie, the amount of which cannot be ascertained.*

The cultivation of tobacco is likely to become a valuable staple of export. Several sugar estates have been purchased by wealthy Cubans, who, abandoning their own distracted island, have settled here. Sir J. P. Grant refers especially to this in his report for 1874, and states that one old sugar estate which was in a languishing

* "Papers relating to Colonial Possessions."—Blue Book, part i. p. 51, 1874.

condition had been purchased by a Cuban gentleman, for which an order for £4,000 worth of new machinery had been given. In August, 1871, there were only 91 acres of this in cultivation; in 1872 there were 304. Since then the acreage has considerably increased.

Perhaps the most important of all the public works hitherto commenced is the one by which it is proposed to irrigate a large tract of country containing 43,000 acres of land, now lying comparatively waste. A commission is empowered to raise sums not to exceed in all £60,000 by debentures, bearing interest at 5 per cent. per annum, guaranteed by the revenues of the colony. There is abundant evidence of improvement everywhere, yet much remains to be done. A bountiful field of undeveloped resources affords bright hopes for future enterprise — a striking commentary upon the prediction that emancipation would prove the ruin of the West Indies.

The condition of the countries in which negro slavery has been abolished is necessarily, with regard both to what has happened and what is impending, a subject of more than usual interest. The anarchical condition of some of the Southern States of America naturally raises the inquiry how things stand in other countries where emancipation has been accomplished; whilst the threatened destruction of the slave system in Cuba, its last great stronghold, produces anxiety as to whether we shall see there the same miserable results as in Louisiana and Hispaniola.

The black slave, when born on an estate, costs little, but he would not work without physical compulsion; hence the necessity of a staff of overlookers. The presence of thousands of Coolies among a redundant native population is a standing proof to the present hour of the constitutional indolence of the negro. There is small doubt that in point of economy free labour in the long run is cheapest, but not that of white people, for they unquestionably degenerate in tropical climates. Possibly in future ages a hybrid race may arise, producing fit inhabitants for those regions, combining the energy of the Northman with the endurance of the African.

It has been urged in palliation of slavery in our colonies, that the cruelty and tyranny which Africans would have undergone in their own country may have equalled anything known in the plantations; and that, moreover, the imported negro might be raised to lighter occupations as domestics, or even be promoted to be overseers. But the race had no cause to rejoice in the dignity conferred upon a few; and it is a well-known fact that the severest taskmasters are the slaves themselves. No doubt in latter years evils were mitigated, and laws were made to restrain the owners from damaging their "chattels;" but "disguise thyself as thou wilt, still, slavery, still thou art a bitter draught."

In an existence so hopeless and irremediable—illumined at best by the faintest rays of Christianity—suicides were frequent. Death had no terrors, being regarded as the passage back to their own country—a refutation to the assertion that their condition was ameliorated by extradition. This sentiment of hopeful return to their country seems, notwithstanding the lapse of centuries, inherent in the negro mind. Its existence is confirmed by the reports lately quoted in the rebellion of 1865, "that the negroes preferred death to other punishments."

To believe that all proprietors of West Indian estates when they came into possession became monsters of avarice and cruelty, is an unreasonable assumption; numerous instances of the affection and devotion of slaves to their owners afford a proof to the contrary. But slaves were at the mercy of the caprice of their owners; many proprietors were absentees, and all admitted the necessity of enforcing discipline among so great a mass of negroes.*

Civilisation and religion, we hope, have made the world more tender-hearted. When we talk of cruelty to the blacks, let us recall what Englishmen did to Englishmen not two hundred years ago. Witness the punishments in James II.'s reign —sentences of whipping from Newgate to Tyburr, and from Tyburn to Newgate, pilloried, fined, and imprisoned for life. Such was Titus Oates's sentence. Again, look at Judge Jeffreys's "Bloody Assize," and the convicts transported to the West Indies, whose only crime was political adherence to the losing side. Those white slaves were worse off than the blacks, whose owners had an interest in their lives. The case of indentured servants was little better—men who voluntarily came out to be hired. An author who wrote in 1740 describes his landing at Kingston: "As we had a great many servants on board, and some of them fine tradesmen, we had soon a number of the

---

* A friend of mine, who went out as a youth to Demerara in 1826, told me that soon after arrival he spoke to a negro on the estate, who stopped working for the moment to reply to him ; the manager happened to pass at the moment, and the negro was ordered to be flogged for leaving off his work. On my friend remonstrating, the only answer he received was, "Discipline must be maintained." In disgust he left the estate.

planters who came to purchase indentures. It was affecting to see the shoal of buyers, and how the poor fellows were made to pass in review before their future tyrants, who looked at them and examined them as if they had been so many horses. Each chose whom he liked best; a good tradesman went off at about £40, and others at £20."* The writer gives farther on " an abstract of the laws now in force in Jamaica" with reference to servants :—

"All servants shall serve according to contract, and where there is none, servants under eighteen, at their arrival in this island, shall serve seven years, and above eighteen, four years, and all convicted felons for the time of their banishment; and at the end of such times shall receive from their master or employer 40s., and a certificate of their freedom.

"A hired labourer or servant that shall embezzle, purloin, or waste his employer's money or goods, shall serve, or make satisfaction, at the discretion of any Justice of Peace; if above the value of 40s. they shall serve two years without wages, and further, in case that time will not satisfy.

"If a man servant marry without his master's consent, he shall serve two years for the offence.

"Servants absenting themselves from their ser-

* "A New History of Jamaica," p. 15.

vice, shall for every day's absence serve one week, and so proportionably for a longer time, the whole not exceeding three years.

"If any servant, through wilful misbehaviour, happens to have the French-pox, yaws, or any other disease, broken bones, sickness, impediment or imprisonment, he or she shall serve double the time thereby neglected, and make good all charges occasioned by reason thereof.

"No servant shall be whipped naked without order from a Justice of Peace," &c., &c.

The "Justices of Peace" were of course planters. Reverting to slaves, Sloane describes the economy and discipline of the estates. "For negligence," he says, "slaves are usually whipped by the overseers with lance-wood switches till they be bloody, and several of the switches broken, being first tied up by their hands in the mill-houses." "After they are whipped till they are raw, some put on their skins pepper and salt to make them smart; at other times their masters will drip melted wax on their skins, and use several very exquisite tortures." So much for negligence! "For running away, they put iron rings of great weight on their ankles, or pottocks about their necks, which are iron rings with two long necks riveted to them, or a spur in the mouth." Some-

times half the foot was cut off by an axe. Rebellion was a capital offence; and the penalty was being slowly burnt to death. The poor wretch was fastened down to the ground, "with crooked sticks on every limb; they then applied fire by degrees, from the feet and hands, burning them gradually up to the head, whereby their pains are extravagant." And the educated writer expresses his opinion, "These punishments are sometimes merited by the blacks, who are a very perverse generation of people; and though they appear harsh, yet are scarce equal to some of their crimes, and inferior to what punishments other European nations inflict on their slaves in the East Indies." *
So much for the gentle rule of the British in 1687.

Now let us glance at the amended laws in George II.'s reign. Here are specimens of paternal government:—

"If a negro slave strikes any person, except in defence of his owner's person or goods, he shall for the first offence be severely whipped by order of a Justice of Peace; for the second, by the like order, be severely whipped, his or her nose slit, and face burnt in some place; and for the third offence, left to two Justices and three freeholders to inflict death, or what other punishment they think fit."

* "Sir Hans Sloane's Voyage," &c., p. lvii.

"No slave shall be free by becoming a Christian, but shall, as to payment of debts, be accounted chattels, and where other chattels are not sufficient, so many slaves as necessary shall be sold for payment of debts. In all other cases, negroes and slaves shall be taken as freehold, and descend accordingly."

This was a most cruel provision of the Imperial Legislature. Slaves formed friendships like other people, and they had their allotted plantations and houses; their love of family and friends was great, and to separate them from all they held dear was to drain the last bitter drop in their cup of misery.

Mr. Bryan Edwards records a scene in good King George III.'s reign, of which he was an eye-witness in 1760. Three Koromantyn negroes were found guilty of murder and insurrection. One was condemned to be burnt, and the other two to be hung up alive in irons, and left to perish in that situation. The wretch that was burnt was made to sit on the ground, and his body being chained to an iron stake, the fire was applied to his feet. He uttered not a groan, and saw his legs reduced to ashes with the utmost composure; one of his arms getting loose, he snatched a brand from the fire and flung it at the face of the executioner. The two that were hung up alive were indulged, at their own request, with a hearty meal before they were suspended on the gibbet, which was erected on the parade at Kingston.

Edwards visited them on the seventh day. The two criminals laughed immoderately at something that occurred. The next morning one of them silently expired, as did the other on the morning of the ninth day.* These circumstances are not mentioned as having excited any feelings of horror, although Mr. Edwards was a very humane person. How would they operate now, when the public mind revolts at the idea of the infliction of twelve lashes on the back of a garotter?

"It is the custom," writes Mr. Edwards, "among some of the planters in Jamaica, to mark the initials of their name on the shoulder or breast of each newly-purchased negro by means of a small silver brand heated in the flame of spirits; but it is growing into disuse."†

The manners of proprietors in other islands were not as they might have been; probably they were no better in Jamaica; the only improvement apparent is, that assaults on slaves were brought under legal cognisance, *e. g.* :—

"At St. Christopher's, Mr. Jordan Burke was indicted for cutting off one ear and slitting the other

* "History of the West Indies," ii. 67.   † Ibid., p. 130.

of his female slave Clarissa, upon the 8th of March, 1785. He was fined £50 currency for the offence."*

Upon the same island, Mr. Wadham Strode was indicted for cutting off one ear and slitting the other of his negro man Peter, 11th May, 1785. Fined £100.

"A merchant of Basse-Terre, St. Christopher's, a Mr. W. Herbert, was found guilty of wounding a negro child called Billy, of the age of six years, and was sentenced to pay a fine of 40s.;" and he actually brought a successful action against the magistrates, denying their authority to interfere. Enough, however, of sickening details, and we may thank our stars that we were born in days of emancipation, for—

>"Children we are all
Of one great Father, in whatever clime
His providence hath cast the deed of life,—
All tongues, all colours! Neither after death
Shall we be sorted into languages
And tints—white, black, and tawny, Greek and Goth,
Northman, and offspring of hot Africa;
The all-seeing Father—He in whom we live and move—
He, the indifferent Judge of all—regards
Nations, and hues, and dialects alike;
According to their works shall they be judged."

---

* Southey, "Chron. Hist.," iii. 8. The difference between Jamaica money and British was 25 *per cent.* £75 sterling makes £100 Jamaica currency.

The "Papers relating to her Majesty's Colonial Possessions" contain, as is usual, information of great value and interest. The condition of these colonies, reported a few years back to be desperate, is now favourable and promising; law and order are perfectly and easily maintained, and the amount of exports and imports indicate industrial growth and commercial improvement Jamaica having presented, perhaps, the example of the lowest depressure, now bids fair to be foremost in revival. Her chief difficulty lies in the inertness of her black natives, habituated by long usage to a low standard of physical comfort. Possessed of a varied climate, and of a fertile soil which will grow literally anything, they are not willing to exert themselves more than is necessary for the bare supply of their immediate wants.

One fact tells a good deal: the sugar crop of Jamaica in 1871 was the largest known for nineteen years. The crop of the next year was a comparative failure; yet the total value of the produce and manufactures of the island amounted to £1,348,858, being upwards of £150,000 more than in the year of the large sugar crop.* This, of course, indicates an increase in other products

* Vide Blue Book for 1874, pp. 54,55.

than that on which the colony used too exclusively to rely. The production of coffee fluctuates considerably, according to the character of the season, but in 1872 it was greater than for many years before. The acreage under tobacco had in one year increased more than threefold. "There is nothing," says the Report, "to prevent Jamaica cigars equalling those exported from Havannah." The value of the fruits exported this year (1874) has more than doubled that of the year before, having been £5,855 as against £2,736; and almost the same may be said of smaller commodities, the only two exceptions being ginger and arrowroot.

The total value of imports for 1872 was £1,559,602, being an increase of 50 per cent., arrived at gradually and steadily within five years. Some of the items of largest increase are very suggestive. In 1866 no steam-engines were imported; in 1872 the value was £14,033. Again, in the former year, the value of mills (sugar) and other machinery imported was £6,908, in the latter £26,809. A proof "that everywhere planters are making efforts, by means of improved machinery and new processes, to improve their manufacture of sugar. This," continues the Report, "is a new feature in the history of Jamaica sugar-planting" (p. 54).

It is also remarkable that a large portion of the new investments in Jamaica are being made by foreigners. "A noted French firm is about to establish a factory for making the extract of logwood in this island." It is also noticeable that the cultivation of tobacco, almost discontinued since the time of the Spaniards, has been restored to a considerable extent by Spaniards. In certain districts "the cultivation of tobacco is carried on mostly by Cubans, who have settled and become the owners of property." In fact, so unskilful or unenergetic had been the management of English planters in Jamaica, that "these lazy Spaniards" have come over to teach us, and are succeeding where we failed. "The skill, industry, and enterprise of these our new fellow-subjects must tell upon their neighbours, and thus, indirectly, must benefit the whole colony." So speaks an English governor of Spaniards.

Sir John Peter Grant left the colony in 1874, and was succeeded in the government by Sir William Grey.

CHAPTER XIII.

SPANISH TOWN AND LINSTEAD.

Thursday, 18th June.—I arose at 5 A.M., for B—— and I have arranged a little excursion. We sent our bags down to "The Gardens" last night by some return mules. Having breakfasted, we mounted our steeds with our water-proofs on, for unfortunately it was raining heavily. We rode down what is called the "Morning Road," which winds round the line of hills on the other side of the valley, and is considered an easier descent than the one by which we had ascended. We passed through coffee plantations, crossed streams, and dived into gorges filled with the same luxuriant vegetation which has been already described.

We reached Bolton's stables in an hour and a half; here we left our horses, entered a four-wheeled two-horse buggy, and drove to Widcomb, the residence of the officer commanding the troops in the island. Orderlies of the 2nd West

India Regiment—tall, stalwart, muscular negroes, in undress Zouave uniform, white linen tunics, blue knickers, and ponderous shoes, with white gaiters—were in readiness to show us into the house, which is beautifully situated, overlooking the flat, or rather the gentle slope, that extends to Kingston. After a most courteous reception by a most hospitable host and hostess, and being refreshed with luncheon, we started again in our buggy for Spanish Town, a distance of sixteen miles.

A level road, in some places rather soft and sandy, but generally well kept, leads to the former metropolis, as uninteresting a flat as can be. To be sure we might have taken the train from Kingston by the only railway in the island, whch runs through Spanish Town, with a terminus at Old Harbour, a line of twenty-six miles; but when I tell you that a gentleman informed me that he arrived for the train advertised to start at 12 o'clock (mid-day), and that he waited at the station till 2 o'clock, and then saw the stoker going out to cut fuel in order to light the engine fire, you will readily perceive why we preferred the road. A lady also told me that having left Spanish Town in the evening for Kingston, she was benighted, and had to pass the remainder of the night, or morning, at a friend's house. I never heard what dividend was paid by the directors on this line. It strikes me as curious that there should be no public horse conveyances on the roads. I refer to stage-coaches. There were, in the last century, public conveyances between Kingston and Spanish Town and Passage Fort, six miles distant. The fare to the latter place was twelve shillings sterling.*

At first we passed properties fenced in with pinguins and dildoes; we then came to monotonous copses of cashaw-trees, the wood of which is here universally used for fuel, and consequently is valuable. Our driver—a tall negro with a cocoanut-shaped head covered with the stiffest wool, and pouting lips of great extension—showed an anxiety to join in our conversation in order to prove to us how much he knew about everything. He told us that leaves of the cashaw are poisonous to cattle, and that if they drink water after eating them recovery is hopeless.

Gentlemen of colour, even my short experience has enabled me to discern, are extremely self-confident and vain. The strut of a negro, male or female, in gay attire, is curious to observe. The woman, probably without shoes or stockings all

* Gardner, p. 164.

the week, with a print skirt and bandana on her head, turns out on Sundays and holidays in rich costume, with all the ease and grace of a lady always accustomed to fine clothes. Yet it must be confessed that there is no appearance of vulgarity; she feels and maintains the dignity due to the appropriation of superior attire.

People often pride themselves on the possession of some quality of which they have the least reason to be proud. So the ignorant negro affects general if not universal knowledge. I must say, that I have invariably found them most good-humoured, civil, and obliging. They are very easily amused; the slightest incident excites their risible faculties. It is sufficient for one to be seen laughing to set off a whole company of negroes into most hearty yah-yahs, although they may not have witnessed the circumstances that gave rise to it. The negro brain is scarcely capable of high culture. The coloured people are sharper, and most of the employés in government and other offices are supplied by this class; but even in these days of liberality of sentiment one cannot but observe a great prejudice against the faintest stain of black blood. The negroes make excellent servants, being attentive and remarkably quiet in their movements, and there are few resident families in which there is not an old and confidential black domestic. A butler's wages may be reckoned at 8s. a week; I believe that is the maximum. A cook's, 6s. to 8s., the latter being those of a professed cook. A housemaid's, 5s. to 6s. It would be presumptuous in me to attempt to delineate the intricacies of negro life and character, I can only repeat what I heard rather than what I saw. It does not, however, require much experience or penetration to detect that the weak points are indolence and untruthfulness. They take pleasure in prayer-meetings and psalm-singing, but their religion cannot be deep-rooted. They are very superstitious; all believe in the existence of *duppies* or ghosts; and the belief in witchcraft, under the name of Obeism and Myalism, a branch of the black art, is not yet stamped out.

In all directions I heard complaints of the difficulty in obtaining labour—a serious impediment to the development of the country's resources. The only labour which is cheerfully performed by the negro in Jamaica is in his own "provision ground." There he works *da cuore*. But, after all, no great labour is required on this productive soil. The average rent of an acre of ground is 20s., and that quantity, or even half an acre, according to the number, is sufficient to maintain a family. There the negro is independent; he is a landowner, and consequently acquires dignity; the bountiful soil produces mangoes, yams, plantains, bananas, chow-chows, bread-fruit, sweet-potatoes, cassava, melons, and gourds, probably cocoanut and castor-oil trees; and with what he is able to sell he purchases pork and salt fish. "*O fortunati agricolæ!*" and they do seem to appreciate their advantages, for they are all merry and lighthearted. The present generation can know but little of the sufferings of their progenitors. The *insouciance* and unreflective temperament of the negro is admirably hit off in the following trait—a sketch from the life, I think in the works of poor Artemus Ward:—

"'My brother,' I sed to a cullerd purson, 'air you aware that you've been mancipated? Do you realise how glorious it is to be free? Tell me, my dear cullerd brother, does it not seem to you like some dream? or do you realise the great fact in all its lovin' and holy magnitood?' He said he would take some gin."

In a pleasant little book on Jamaica, which was lent to me while I was in the island, written in 1873 by a traveller who evidently kept his ears and eyes open, I read, what I should believe to be a correct analysis of negroes generally :—

"A man's estimate of the negro character varies according to the length of time he spends among them. The first year, his opinion of them is a high one. He is amused by their merry faces, their broad grins, their apparent good nature, their seeming simplicity of character. He looks upon them as happy children, for whom the song, and the dance, and the church constitute the essentials of life. The second year, his ideas are somewhat modified. He regards them as children still, but now as spoiled children, who give a great deal of trouble; and by the third or fourth year, he has begun to talk about the 'irrepressible nigger,' and to speak of them in very much the same language as the planters get the credit of doing."*

The importation of Coolies has greatly diminished the evil attendant on a non-working native community. The Government exercises a most paternal supervision over the emigration and immigration of these British subjects; and officials are specially appointed to watch over their interests and comforts. There are difficulties in obtaining a consignment of Coolies; application for them must be made of course through the

* "Letters from Jamaica," p. 80.

Government. I think not less than twenty-five can be applied for; and the applicant has to prove that he possesses means for their pay, subsistence, lodging, and for a hospital in case of sickness. On their arrival, they are indentured or apprenticed for five years; the number of hours and days of labour, and the rate of wages, are all made conditions with the Government Inspector. They are hard working and steady, saving all they can. I never heard of a single complaint of the conduct of these Orientals from any proprietor; both sides are satisfied, for the Coolie generally indentures for another term. After ten years' service, if he desires to return to his native country, he is entitled to a free passage; in many instances he returns accompanied by others of his countrymen, whom his representations have induced to emigrate and improve their condition.

I have been a long time getting over this ground, almost as long as if we had taken tickets in the Kingston and Spanish Town express train, and all through our driver's imparting some curious information about cashaw-trees. He now addressed us again, and advised us to smoke, as we have to traverse a swamp for some miles. Stagnant water lay on either side of us, in appearance a planted lagune; but I could not see far through it on account of the thick brushwood: giant rushes and water-lilies decorated the roadside pools. Here must fever and ague perpetually incubate; and yet there are habitations here and there, and on the harder portions of ground roads have been formed, leading probably to the dwelling-places of the woodmen.

By-the-bye, I made a cutting from the *Times* of May 27, 1874, containing an account of the blue gum tree. I wonder how it would answer here:—

"THE BLUE GUM TREE.—The *San Francisco Bulletin* states that, in California, there have now been planted, probably, not less than a million of these trees, which have become so famous for draining damp soils, and for destroying malaria. The *Eucalyptus globulus* is an evergreen, a native of Tasmania, remarkable for rapid growth, attaining a *maximum* height of about 300 ft., with a circumference of from 30 to 50 ft. The leaves are about ten inches long, an inch wide, exhaling a strong camphor-like odour. The timber is hard, easily worked, and very serviceable for keels of vessels, bridges, and other uses where strength and durability are essential. The tree supplies a medicinal preparation, efficacious in throat affections and intermittent fever. The *Bulletin* says, that near Haywards, in California, about 150,000 of these trees were planted by the Surveyor-General, and though they are only about five years old, many are 40 ft. or 50 ft. high."

At no great distance farther on we stopped to gaze with wonder at an enormous Ceiba, or Cotton-tree, which grew on one side of the road. I had seen several in my rides about Newcastle, but never one of such dimensions as this; and I am not sure that this is the largest in the island. We could not calculate its girth, for a hedge-row prevented circumambulation; but we paced the shade cast down by its branches on the road, under a vertical sun, and it measured sixty yards. Its branches grow horizontally, and each of them would be considered in England a good-sized tree. In order to support the superincumbent weight of the branches, Nature (as we express ourselves), in her wonderful providence, has supplied these trees with buttresses, which project laterally from the trunk, and are so prominent that a person might shelter himself between them. The timber of these trees is valueless; the only use made of the great arms is for canoes, which the negroes still employ on the rivers and creeks; and probably the great canoes which Columbus described were formed from these trees. The blossoms, which have a woolly or cottony appearance, are said to be available for stuffing cushions and mattresses.

The negroes regard this tree with superstitious reverence, and believe that if a person throw a stone at the trunk he will surely be visited by sickness or some other misfortune; and when they intend to cut one down, they first pour rum at the root as a propitiatory offering.

The botanical name of this tree is Eriodendron, literally wool-tree, and it is one of the few deciduous trees in the island; for, in general, a tropical forest knows no such phenomenon as the fall of the leaf—that is, the decay of some and the unfolding of other leaves proceed simultaneously and constantly, so that the foliage is ever full and verdant.* "It is not uncommon," continues Gosse, "for the trunk of the Ceiba to reach one hundred feet in naked majesty before a single branch is put out; and not unfrequently one hundred and fifty feet." If we are to believe a statement I read in a publication called *The Garden*, some of the specimens of the *Eucalyptus amygdalina* in Australia, measured by Baron von Müller, the Government botanist of Victoria, would overtop the cross on St. Paul's Cathedral.

* "Naturalist in Jamaica," p. 277.

These heights remind me of the trees in Wisconsin of which I have heard, as being so tall that it takes two men and a boy to look to the top of them. One looks till he gets tired, and another commences where he left off.

We passed a grand house of Mr. Levi, a Government contractor, with numbers of cattle—fine-looking beasts—in the grounds or pen. All country properties are called Pens out here; where sugar is grown they are called Estates. Perhaps the designation Pen originated from a custom mentioned by Sloane: "Cattle are penn'd every night, or else they in a short time would run wild."

We crossed a fine bridge, and shortly after we entered Spanish Town, situated on the banks of the Cobre, at the extremity of a vast plain, bounded by the Cedar Valley Mountains on the north and north-west; it is thirteen miles from Kingston, and six from the sea at Port Henderson and Passage Fort. We drove through the deserted streets of the former capital, passing many half-closed stores, and several spacious houses in a state of dilapidation. How fallen down since the time of the proud Spaniard and the palmy days of San Iago de la Vega! and after it became plain Spanish Town, we may still fancy the vivacity and gaiety imported into the place, when the Governor resided and his Council met there, and the forty-seven members of the House of Assembly, with the captains, the judges, the treasurers, and the custodes of the parishes. We may fancy the session in progress, and the wives and families who accompanied the magnates, and think what dinners were given, with what a consumption of turtle, land-crabs, and Madeira.

Large houses, which once resounded with merriment, music, and dancing, are now silent and tottering, their walls defaced with cracks, or their windows partly boarded up, with a black face here and there peering out: cheap lodgings there, no doubt. The sounds of wheels in the streets are rare, I presume; we heard none but our own. How different the description of an eye-witness who wrote in 1740: "'Tis surprising to see the number of coaches and chariots which are perpetually plying, besides those which belong to private persons." He goes on to say, "They have frequent balls, and lately have got a play-house where they retain a set of extraordinary good actors." *

The Government buildings (or a portion of them) are now converted into a college. B—— was

* "A New History of Jamaica," p. 27.

acquainted with the Principal, and had written to ask his hospitality for a night. His answer was to be sent to the post-office, Gordon Town, "to be kept till called for." We called there for it, but the postmaster had neglected his instructions, and had forwarded it with other letters to Newcastle. Our driver pulled up at what he told us was the college gate, but it was fastened. Nobody being at hand to inform us, we alighted, and seeing a crowd a little way off, we pushed through it, and, curious to ascertain the cause, we entered a lofty hall, and found that the sessions were going on. The staircase was crowded with ascending and descending negroes, and women blocked up the way, seated with baskets of fruit. I saw grapes, mangoes, and avocado pears. One of them, in reply to our salutation, thrust forward her infant: "Fine baby, sar, all my own, sar!" She was, I presume, on the look out for a gratuity —a "quattie" or a "bit;"* but I must say I was never asked for anything during my visit. We entered the crowded court, where Mr. Justice Bruce was presiding in wig and gown. I could have remained and listened to the proceedings, which no doubt would have been highly amusing, but we had announced that our arrival at the college

* A "quattie" is a penny-halfpenny; a "bit" fourpence-halfpenny.

would be at luncheon-time; and we received keen warnings of that vacuum disapproved of by private individuals as well as by nature, so we descended. I made my way into the post-office, and asked a coloured clerk to direct us. Scarcely looking up, he said he had not time to answer me. I felt what the French would call a *crispation* in my fingers and feet, but I walked out. At last some one condescended to tell us that we must drive round to the principal entrance. So away we went through a narrow street, and then emerged in a handsome square. If this was designed by the Spaniards, they had grand notions. Public buildings coloured yellow on each side, in the midst a garden, with a flagstaff in the centre. Our buggy landed us at a flight of steps under an imposing-looking Ionic portico; this was King's House, or rather the entrance to it. A black butler answered our appeal at the bell.

"Is Mr. Chadwick at home?"

"Yes, but he is very ill, three days in bed."

B—— expressed his regret, and said he had written to propose a visit, but that now we had better go. The butler thought so too. B—— then inquired if he could get us any refreshment; he said he could, and we entered the house. He led us through a spacious hall, and wide passages, with polished mahogany floors, up a fine staircase, and then, in a long corridor, we found two black women-nurses. We walked on tip-toe, and the head nurse spoke in a whisper that Mr. Chadwick was very ill with dysentery, and must be kept very quiet. He was fed every two hours with strong soups and champagne, and the doctor thought him rather better that morning. Then we were shown into what had evidently been the Governor's or his Lady's drawing-room, the handsome furniture still remaining. The Gætulian Ganymede, I mean the black butler—

>"tu Gætulum Ganymedem
>Respice, quum sities :"—Juv.

appeared with a decanter of claret and a plate of crackers, to which we were addressing our attention, when the nurse entered and said Mr. Chadwick had expressed a wish to see the Captain. So B—— went, and came back reporting that the invalid was suffering from great weakness.

Then Mr. Grant Allen, the Vice-Principal, appeared, and explained that there had been a mistake about the letter which was to have been sent to tell us the state of the case, and he kindly offered to show us the lions of the place. King's House is really a fine edifice, better inside than out, I should say, for the façade does not present much architectural beauty. There is a large, well-proportioned ball-room in it, the dimensions being about 70 feet by 30 feet, and the height about 32 feet, and at one end are portraits of George III. and his Queen. The History to which I have just before alluded states that "the Governor's house is of stone; it was lately rebuilt by the Duke of Portland" (p. 29). The other three sides of the square included all the buildings requisite for carrying on the public business of the island, such as the House of Assembly, County Court, &c. At one end of the northern range was the Arsenal and Guard-house, at the other the offices of the Island Secretary; in the centre is a temple, with a cupola and lanthorn supported on open arches, within which was placed a statue of Lord Rodney, commemorative of his glorious victory over the French fleet on the 12th of April, 1782. This temple is connected with the other buildings by a not ungraceful semicircular colonnade on either side. The statue was executed in England by the elder Bacon at a cost of £3,000, and has now been removed to Kingston, another burning indignity to the Spanish Town folk. Above the arches are some commendatory lines in Latin, with the arms of the gallant Admiral in white plaster upon the yellow stucco.

In front of the temple are placed two long bronze French 32-pounder guns, trophies doubtless of that day, probably taken out of the *Ville de Paris*. They bear the inscription, "LOUIS CHARLES DE BOURBON, COMPTE D'EU DUC D'AUMALE, 4TH MAY, 1748." On the chase of one was its name, "LE PRECIPICE," on the other "LE MODESTE," and on each, "ULTIMA RATIO REGUM." Many other guns are lying about there, some of them doing duty as posts.

The parterre in the middle of the square, once no doubt the rendezvous of the *élite* of the town when military bands played there, is now, like the rest, in a neglected state. Choice trees and shrubs are still in luxuriance there, and many a garden flower now grows wild. I inquired the name of a peculiar looking tree growing there, and was told it was the Sandbox (*Hura crepitans*), and I was afterwards presented with one of the seeds, or pods, which are round, parted into most symmetrical divisions, like those of an orange. When ripe the pod bursts, exploding with the noise of a pistol shot, and scattering its seeds all about. Why called Sandbox I cannot imagine, unless from its similarity to those boxes from which sand was powdered to dry up ink (instead of using blotting-paper), such as we may still see in France.

The allusion to the *élite* of the town reminds me of a passage in the "History of Jamaica" (A.D. 1740), so often before quoted. You will agree that fashionable clothing was cool, but not graceful.

"The common dress here is none of the most becoming. The heat makes many clothes intolerable, and therefore the men generally wear only thread stockings, linen drawers and vest, a handkerchief tied round their head, and a hat above. Wigs are never used but on Sundays or in court-time; and then gentlemen appear very gay in silk coats and vests trimmed with silver. The servants wear a coarse Osnaburg frock, long trousers of the same, a speckled shirt, and no stockings. Negroes go mostly naked, except those who attend gentlemen, who have them dressed in their own livery, though 'tis the utmost pain to the uneasy slave.

"The ladies are as gay as anywhere in Europe, dress as richly, and appear with as good a grace. Their morning habit is a loose night-gown, carelessly wrapped about them; before dinner they get out of their deshabille, and show themselves in all the advantage of a becoming rich, neat dress. The servant-maids have generally a linen or striped holland gown, and plain head-cloths. The negro-women go, many of them, quite naked; they do not know what shame is, and are surprised at an European's bashfulness, who perhaps turns his head aside at the sight. Their masters give them a kind of petticoat, but they do not care to wear it. In the towns they are obliged to do it" (p. 35).

"Oh! what a blessed thing it is," ejaculated Squeers, "to be in a state of natur'!"

Mr. Grant Allen told us that there were no objects of antiquity in the place; that the long ungainly-looking brick church which we had passed on entering the town—the Cathedral, by-the-bye—with the exception of a few monuments, was not worth seeing.* We were, however, *en route* for it, when a servant ran out to say that Mrs. Allen was waiting luncheon for us. Here was an agreeable surprise, and we were brisk in obeying the summons. A very pleasant repast it was, and the impromptu manner in which it was prepared made the pleasure greater.

---

* The church was rebuilt in two years at the parochial expense, on the site of the former one, irreparably damaged by the hurricane of August, 1712, and probably on the site of the Spanish Red Cross Church.

"Grata superveniet quæ non sperabitur hora,"

so Horace expresses himself, as no doubt you are aware. The collation required no apology; but our kind entertainers informed us of the difficulty in supplying a table, for, now that Spanish Town is so poorly inhabited, fish and other provisions are carried past it to Linstead, where well-to-do native proprietors are proving good customers.

The late energetic Governor, Sir J. P. Grant, perhaps as some indemnity to the deserted metropolis, conceived the idea of utilising the abandoned public offices by converting them into a grand College, which might attract pupils from all the West Indian Islands. With this view two Professors, distinguished in honours at Oxford, were selected as Principal and Vice-Principal; a third permanent officer was retained as a steward and secretary, also at a liberal salary. The Governor's former official residence constitutes the Professors' quarters, the examination hall, the refectory, the kitchens, and the servants' rooms of the College. Other public offices have been converted into dormitories, ready with every necessary for the immediate reception of occupants, and into lecture-rooms fitted with every scientific instrument, and capable of holding several hundreds. And how many pupils do you suppose have been attracted hitherto by this powerful and eminent staff, these scientific apparatus, and these preparations for resident comfort? Three coloured youths!

The fact is, those who can afford to send their sons out of their islands for education would at once unhesitatingly send them to England for the *prestige* thereto appertaining, although the education might be superior here.

Acting on poor Mr. Chadwick's advice, we went to call on Sir Bryan Edwards, late Chief Justice of Jamaica; so we re-entered our buggy and were driven to his residence, "Eltham Pen," about two miles from Spanish Town. Sir Bryan is the nephew of the author of the "History of the West Indies." I abominate that new word and custom which has come to us in England across the Atlantic, "interviewing." My feeling is, that where one is admitted into the society of another, there is a tacit honourable understanding that all communications are privileged, and every look and gesture are not to be recorded for publication. This applies generally, for there was nothing special whatever in this case.

Sir Bryan dines at four; it was now past five, and he was out walking in his grounds, which seemed very pretty. His servant went to seek him. When he arrived he received us with those easy, friendly manners which seem to be part of the constitution of the island, so that we were at our ease at once, and felt as if an old acquaintance were being renewed. We obtained some useful *renseignements* for our journey, and being anxious to have time and light to inspect the "Bogue-walk," a celebrated locality, we shortly took our leave, Sir Bryan kindly expressing a wish that we would revisit him.

Jogging onwards, we passed the extensive works which are being constructed for irrigation purposes, another improvement introduced I believe by Sir J. P. Grant. We hope to have another look at them. We have gone over about six miles of ground, I should judge, since we left Spanish Town, driving through a fine open country, and the scenes changes. We are entering a gorge, crossing a bridge rightly called Flat Bridge, and just beyond there are some ancient walls, erected, according to tradition, by the Spaniards—the remains, no doubt, of a fortress which guarded the defile—and this is the Bogue-walk. Bog or Bogue from the Spanish *Boca*, a mouth. Walk is an expression often used here to denote certain localities; for example, the "Walk's Road," "Seven-mile Walk," the present Kent

Village, just seven miles from Spanish Town, and "Sixteen-mile Walk," on the road northward over Mount Diablo; and the expression was perhaps derived from the times when a traveller, whether on foot or horseback, would find himself reduced to a walk, in consequence of either the badness or the steepness of the road.

The Cobre,* with the confluence of the Rio Negro and d'Oro, twists and winds like the coils of a snake—babbling and hissing over rocks, reminding one of favourite salmon leaps in the Scotch waters. The scenery is beautiful. A limestone mountain seems to have been split in twain, the river sides, precipitous as can be, having in the lapse of ages become clothed with foliage of every variety of form and grandeur and tint. The river has made its way at the base, the road is formed on one side, on a level, and parallel with its windings, the stream being retained in its channel, where necessary, by a stone parapet.

Along the banks are massed in elegant and

---

* *Cobre* (Spanish and Portuguese), copper. It has been imagined that the Spaniards gave it that name from passing through a vein of that metal. Blome and other early writers assert that there were mines of silver and copper, and Edwards believed the fact. Others, again, have conjectured that the original name was Cobra, Portuguese for snake, apparently more appropriate from its serpentine course.

dense confusion specimens, I should think, of all the foliage of the island—varieties of tree-ferns, palms, and palmettoes, with their broad fan-like leaves, bamboos being most conspicuous and ornamental. These noble reeds, often fifty feet high, are exceedingly graceful, and are grouped like Prince of Wales's feathers. If one can imagine a circlet of green ostrich feathers of that dimension, you will have some idea of them. The lower formation of the rocky sides is curiously honeycombed; we got out to examine it, and to gather some specimens of ferns and flowers.

A romantic and delightful drive, it is the high road from Spanish Town to the parish of St. Thomas-in-the-Vale, and generally to the north side of the island, so that there were many wayfarers, women carrying burdens as usual on their heads. At one wind we came upon a group, some seated on the parapet, others in the road, all chatting and laughing. The bright hues of their clothing have a picturesque effect; I begin to think black people are more in keeping with such scenery than the pale-faced whites. Now and then a Coolie passes us, in white clothing and turban; he respectfully salaams with grace and dignity and serious demeanour, so unlike the grinning, teeth-displaying negro. Then a ponderous wain came along, loaded with, I presume, hogsheads of sugar, attended by several drivers, and drawn by twelve oxen.

We lingered over this charming scenery, which extends for about four miles; we now emerge, and are in the midst of green fields and rich pasturages of guinea-grass. This valuable esculent grows luxuriantly in all parts of the island; it thrives even in stony and sterile soils. No anxieties are entertained here about the prospect of the hay harvest, or whether the grain-crops will be short of straw. There is a perpetual reaping of guinea-grass, a food in which horses and cattle delight, and on which they thrive. The account given of its introduction here is as follows:—

"About the year 1744 the seeds of the guinea-grass were brought from the coast of Guinea to Jamaica, to feed some birds brought as presents to Mr. Ellis, Chief Justice of the island. Fortunately the birds died, and the remainder of the seeds were thrown away within a fence, where they grew. The eagerness of the cattle to eat the grass suggested the idea of cultivating it; and a vast advantage has been derived from so doing: it thrives in the most rocky places, and thus renders lands productive which had been considered of no value.*"

Mr. Gosse states that an estate called Shuttlewood (in the vicinity of Montego Bay) was pointed out to him as being the ground where the birdseeds were thrown out.

We are traversing what appears to be a rich agricultural district. Comfortable-looking residences, painted white and green, with accompanying jalousies, are frequent on each side of the road. Some of the residences of the poor "irrepressibles" which we have passed to-day are of the meanest description—wattles for walls and palm-leaves for roof, and there's the house.

We passed some extensive tobacco plantations, on ground lately purchased by Cubans.

I think that it was about 7 o'clock when we drove into Linstead, one of the many flourishing villages which have sprung up since emancipation. We passed some stores and a bazaar, then we turned to the left and entered a parallel street or lane, and pulled up at the little inn, a one-storied bungalow in a garden. Perceiving some inmates at table, we inquired somewhat anxiously if we could have beds; and being answered affirma-

* Southey's "Chron. Hist. of the West Indies," ii. 300.

tively, we brought out our bags, and the buggy and horses went round to the yard.

There was a saloon in front, and a small room off it at the back for meals. We could have only one bedroom, and that not a spacious one, entered from the saloon. It contained one very low bedstead, a crib in fact, and a ponderous four-poster. The contrast between the two was remarkable. The latter, I guess, had been purchased at a sale from some great house, for the posts were of massive carved mahogany. We asked for anything they could give us to eat; and we shortly sat down to coffee and ham and eggs.

We got into conversation with our fellow-guests; they consisted of an elderly gentleman and his daughter, proceeding to Black-river Bay, and another gentleman with his wife, who had been nine years in Kingston, and was now taking his first outing. The ladies soon retired, and an invitation to the gentlemen to join in a drink immediately put us on easy terms. We gathered much local information from them. We sat out afterwards in the porch, for it was a lovely night, not a breath stirring; but soon we were reduced to our own company, for the other travellers were to start at daybreak. The temperature here is very different to that which we have left behind at the hills. I don't know the state of the thermometer, as there was none to consult, but it would have shown a high figure.

Then to our dormitory. B—— pressed the acceptance of the big bed on me, and assisted me in fastening up some mosquito curtains which I had brought from Newcastle on the saddle-bow. We had many a good laugh at the difficulty in climbing up to this elevated couch. It recalled to my memory one of Dean Ramsay's stories of a country minister who was invited with his wife to pass the night at the house of one of his lairds. The host was very proud of an exceedingly large bed in his ancestral mansion, and in the morning asked the lady how she had slept in it. "O vary well, sir; but indeed, I thought I'd lost the minister a-thegither."

B—— was soon asleep; not so I, the heat was so oppressive, and the noises incessant both within and without the walls. When I tell you that the partitions of the rooms did not rise to the ceiling, and that consequently everything could be heard within the house, and that everybody was snoring, you may form some notion of the distracted state of a sleepless mortal. At the back and side of the house is a paved yard;

horses are not tied up at night, but roam about at their free-will. I heard their hoofs clattering on the stone steps (for we had a door at the back) and expected every moment a horse's head pushed in at the door or window. If in a facetious mood, I dare say you would call this a *nightmare*. Then the village dogs! There was one wretch, a stentorian cur, who would not be quiet, baying the moon perhaps. How I set my teeth and longed to be near him with a revolver or a whip (provided he were chained). He set the others off; every inhabitant of the village must own several dogs. There is a momentary stillness: I entertain a hope—no, bow-wow again, and off goes the chorus far and near. Oh! these " voices of the night," of which Longfellow sang so sweetly, but which were so annoying to me. Besides the inevitable evening concert of chirping things, there were odd sounds of night birds occasionally, possibly owls, but it was a strange hooting noise; so what with owls and howls, horses and snorers, "making night hideous," it is provoking to look down upon that B—— in his lowly pallet, sleeping undisturbed.

I was just falling off, when the early village cock gave timely warning of the coming morn, and all his hens come forth to cackle; then other cocks sound the reveillé, and disgusting ducks awakened commence a paddling noise, and dibble with their beaks in the slush. Oh! the discomfort of a sleepless night—

>Πότνια, πότνια νυξ,
>υπνοδότειρα τῶν πολυπονων βροτῶν
>Ερεβοθεν ἴθι.

At daybreak, too, the coloured maid opens the jalousies of the saloon, and the travellers enter for their coffee before starting.

Friday, 19*th June.*—As I lie on my elevated couch, drowsily looking out through the open windows, what a garden I see before me! Tall palms and cocoanuts, palmistes in variety, plantains and the ubiquitous mango; a beautiful pimento stands prominent, its dark green leaves speckled with bunches of white blossoms, so that when a little breeze, like the breath of zephyr, agitates its branches, the air is filled with fragrance, which is wafted towards me like—

> "Sabean odours from the spicy shore
> Of Araby the blest."

B—— having enjoyed a good night's sleep is dressed and gone, and I hear him at the open window of the saloon in conversation with a native lady who is doing the laundry work of the adjoining cottage. Her ringing laughter is pleasant to hear, and their discourse was most amusing.

I wish I could have written it down. It had reference to a certain black individual who had just walked away, after a long, animated, and loud palaver over the gate. B——, after the usual "morning, mam," asked if that was her intended. She professed to treat this as an excellent joke. Several smart passages of wit occurred on both sides. The conversation ended by the lady quoting one of the quaint negro proverbs: "Nanny-goat neber scratch him back till him see wall;" intimating thereby, so I gathered, that there were obstacles in the way, and with some loud yah-yahs! she, I believe, re-entered the cottage.

Our original design had been, after visiting Spanish Town, to make our way across the country to St. Ann's Bay on the north side of the island, and along the coast, and so back to Newcastle, describing pretty nearly a circle. We now found that it would consume more time than B——'s military duties would allow, and as there were no other means of conveyance for him, we were obliged to return over the same ground. It was a disappointment, for it would have opened up to view a different style of country; the north coast, too, I hear, is rich in diversified scenery. It would have been interesting also to have been on the track of Columbus and the first colonists, and to have seen the remains of grandeur of Sevilla Nueva, the first capital, which I have Sir Bryan Edwards's authority for saying are still visible—the only relics of antiquity, I believe, in the island.

However, there was no help for it; so the only thing to be done was to pay the bill and retrace our steps. I thought the charges high for the accommodation, in fact about the same as at a decent hotel in England. Again *en* buggy, we drove through the beautiful Bog-walk, getting out when anything attracted our attention, and gathering more specimens of ferns and grasses.

We stopped at the the irrigation works. The sun was blazing hotly. Protected by a white umbrella and puggree, it was as much as I could bear, with the addition of the glare from the white concrete of the dams. The intelligent superintendent, an Englishman, received us kindly, and took much trouble to explain the details. The plan is to dam the stream of the Cobre and to raise it in a canal above the level of the land, whence by branch outlets it may be distributed over the arid plains. It is a grand design, to which every one must heartily wish success, although irritation works would be as appropriate a designation as irrigation in some quarters, for

I understand there was an island ràte imposed in order to raise funds for their completion, which has caused some dissatisfaction, thereby arousing many to predict that they will result in failure. The works have been thirteen months in construction, and will require many yet before completion.

We repaired to a wooden edifice kept by an Englishman, late foreman of the works, where refreshments are procurable. He was invalided by rheumatism. We ordered what the place could supply, and having invited the superintendent to join us, and in company with the Government inspector whom we found there, we passed half an hour pleasantly in practical conversation. Having recommended the landlord to try lime-juice for his ailment, we proceeded on our way.

We alighted at the Cotton-tree, which B—— was desirous of sketching, whilst the carriage went on for a change of horses, as we had neared the pen where Bolton turns out his horses.

We came up with some men loading a cart with cocoanuts, from which they were chipping off the rind or husk with the object, I presume, of packing them more closely. The rind is green and soft, like that of a cucumber or melon, though afterwards it becomes the hard shell and fibre of which coir is made. One of the men broke off the head of a nut at my request; the fresh juice, or milk, was sweet, but sowewhat mawkish. He told me the nuts were worth 1s. 6d. a dozen.

The horses having been caught and harnessed, we drove on. We called at the College to inquire after Mr. Chadwick, and were informed that he was slightly better.*

With much dust and heat we reached "The Gardens." Bolton charged four guineas for the buggy and horses, which is certainly a handsome price. I remunerated our driver, who had given us satisfaction; he had made no difficulty about the horses going farther in one day than was expected, and at Linstead he had "valeted" us, and had bestowed upon us all his stock of information. Our own steeds had returned to Newcastle, so we had to call upon Bolton for a supply. There were none in the stables, but a couple were sent for somewhere, and arrived after a considerable lapse of time—miserable-looking, jaded animals. Duval, the active superintendent of the stables, aware of their incapability or infirmities, lent us a pair of spurs. But even with these persuaders B——'s nag every now and then came to a standstill, and

---

* I am sorry to say he sunk under this attack, and died shortly after I left the island.

had it not been for an officer returning to Newcastle, who was provided with a hunting-whip, and who belaboured the flanks of the poor beast, I don't know how we should have got home. At the little village of Middleton there is a bridge, on the parapet of which most of the male population—men and boys—were lounging, taking their ease after the labours of the day. Just at the middle of the bridge B——'s Bucephalus came to a dead stop; the hunting-whip being gone on in front, B—— dug with his heels into the flanks of the animal, he rose in his stirrups and worked at the bit, he prodded the nag's ribs with the point of his umbrella, but all to no purpose. The shouts and laughter of the assembled negroes at every fresh effort of the unfortunate B—— were stunning; they narrowly escaped tumbling over the dwarf walls, their "nateral conwulsions," as Sam Weller would have said, were so violent. We, too, were convulsed with laughter; and it was only by the return of the good-natured owner of the hunting-whip that B—— was enabled to make a start; and so in the dark we reached Newcastle.

CHAPTER XIV.

PLANTS, VEGETABLES, AND ANIMALS. KINGSTON AND PORT ROYAL. "THE NILE" AGAIN.

Sunday, June 21.—This is my last Sunday here, and the last anything has generally something sad about it. I enjoyed the early dip in the swimming-bath, and then we had to hurry down to the barracks for Divine Service. In the afternoon I called to take leave of my many pleasant acquaintances; then we took a final walk up the hill that rises precipitously from our huts. We scrambled up through the close brushwood, and descended in places where we had to lay hold of branches in order to keep our footing; and then, sitting out on an overhanging rock, we viewed the country round. The panoramic glance repaid the struggle. Later I repaired to the tea-table of a gentle lady, who had ordered cassava cakes for my especial edification.

I am disappointed in the fruits of the island.

Avocado pears I did not fancy—a taste to be acquired, I presume, for I see them constantly eaten with apparently great relish. Pine-apples are abundant, and can be purchased at from 3*d.* to 9*d.* each. There are two sorts, cowboys or sugar-pines and ripleys, of which the latter are the best; but they are not equal to English hot-house pines. Shaddocks are like large stringy acid oranges. Mangoes are sickly things; and bananas combine the taste of butter, tallow-candles, and sleepy-pears. There are a variety of other fruits: oranges, limes, tamarinds, guavas, custard-apples, and many others, some of which, I dare say, I never saw or heard of.

I can scarcely leave this subject without alluding to the sugar-cane, one of the most valuable productions of the soil, which has exercised so powerful an influence on the destinies of the West Indies. Its cultivation has been the cause of misery to hundreds of thousands, by the necessary demand of labour—black labour entirely. I am not enlightened on the subject; if you require the information—which I do not suppose you do—it is easy to be obtained from encyclopædias. I wish to speak only from personal observation. I know its botanical name, *arundo saccharifera;* and it has a reedy appearance, several shoots or canes growing from one stem generally to a height of five or six feet, jointed at intervals all the way up, and terminating in long sharp leaves or blades. When the leaves at the joints decay and the cane turns yellow, the plant has attained its maturity. It is cut down, stripped of its top leaves (which are fattening fodder for cattle), and taken to the mills. The juice has then, of course, to be expressed. The crushing process seemed very simple; but from the large importation of steam-engines of late years, great improvements must take place in the entire system of sugar-making. After evaporation, the syrup which is not condensed is filtered away, and the sugar in this state is called RAW, or MUSCOVADO. When further purified, it takes the name of LOAF. Sugar-candy is formed by dissolving loaf-sugar over a fire, boiling it to a syrup, and then exposing it to crystallize in a cool place. The filtered syrups become molasses or treacle; the liquor distilled from the fermented juice or molasses yields the rum so dear to the British tar; and when sliced pine-apples are placed in the puncheons, it becomes the pine-apple rum so dear to the Rev. Mr. Stiggins. Crop time is from January to August, and a friend tells me the average yield of sugar is one hogshead per acre. Bryan Edwards writes, that in the most favourable soil for the growth of the cane, which in Jamaica is called *brick-mould* (not as resembling brick in colour, but as containing a mixture of clay and sand), plant-canes have been known in very fine seasons to yield two tons and a half of sugar per acre, and that a pound of sugar from a gallon of raw liquor is reckoned in Jamaica very good yielding.* I will say no more lest I show my ignorance, and you hereafter retort with a *tu quoque*, that I am like the negro, making the most of my little knowledge.

Most of the European vegetables can be raised in the mountain districts of the island. Those of native growth which came under my notice were chocko, usually called chow-chow, an excellent esculent, very like vegetable-marrow; calalue, a substitute for spinach, and which enters largely into the composition of the famous "pepper-pot"

---

* He further states that, "in Jamaica, the usual mode of calculating, in a general way, the average profits of a sugar estate is to allow £10 sterling per annum for every negro, young and old, employed in this line of cultivation; according to which Mr. Beckford's income, arising from 2,533 negroes, ought to be £25,330 sterling. I doubt, however, as he does not reside in the island, if he has received, on an average of ten years together, anything near that sum; but even this is but 6½ per cent. on his capital, which is £380,000, negroes being one-third of the property, and are usually valued at £50 sterling round" (ii. pp. 205, 256).

—a culinary concoction, by the way, as old as Sloane's time; he refers to "oglios or pepper-pots"—chirimoya, sweet potatoes, and others. Smiling little negro children used to come round to the huts with baskets of vegetables and fruit for sale, with their invariable salutation of "marnin, missus," or "marnin, sar." By-the-bye, we in England believe that a negro always addresses a "buckra" as "massa;" now I never heard the term used out here, although I am told it is freely used in the more retired districts. Occasionally a well-known character—Mother Gordon, a dried-faced, white-haired old negress, accompanied by her young daughters or relations, really handsome women—would call and offer pines and other articles of commerce. She is also a "medicine woman," and would spurt out with volubility the catalogue of diseases she could cure, which included every complaint under the sun; but as she was not over choice in her nomenclature, we always refrained from putting her through her catechism when ladies were present. To see the weird-like crone resting with her hands upon her long pimento staff higher than herself, and the young ones seated on the steps or ground in costumes of many bright colours, and bandanas on their heads, formed a group for the pencil of an artist.

The trees of the island are of great variety and beauty. I am not going to enumerate or describe them. Pimento, mahogany, cedar, papaw, lignum vitæ, the numerous family of palms, and so on. I will only observe that there is scarcely a tree more beautiful or more fragrant than a young pimento about the month of June. Branching on all sides, richly clad with deep green leaves, relieved by an exuberance of white, aromatic flowers, it grows to the height of twenty feet and upwards. The berries become that culinary article all-spice, so called because their flavour is said to resemble a mixture of cinnamon, nutmeg, and cloves. The small branches are well known in England, as forming umbrella and walking sticks.

Evelyn states in his diary for the 12th of February, 1672 : "At the Council, we entered on inquiries about improving the plantations, &c., and considered how nutmegs and cinnamon might be obtained and brought to Jamaica, that soil and climate promising success." Whether they did anything more than "consider" does not appear; but Dallas states that "plants of the genuine cinnamon, taken in a vessel bound to Europe from the Isle of France, were presented to the Government of Jamaica by Lord Rodney in

1782. By slips from these plants many thousand trees of it have been cultivated."*

Sea and land turtle are plentiful; so are oysters, cray-fish, and land-crabs. Turtle is sold at 6*d.* *per* lb. The oysters are small, and are usually found attached to the roots and stems of mangroves, which, extending themselves into the sea, are fastened upon by the oysters. This has given rise to the popular error that the oysters grow upon trees. Of crustacea, the most deservedly prized is the land-crab. It may be considered the *cordon bleu* of all the delicacies of the Land of Streams. There are two or three species; one is distinguished by the name of the mountain-crab. The habits of these animals are so curious, that I extract the following account of them from " Edwards's History " (i. 97). Mr. Bryan Edwards wrote in 1793, and says: "The mountain-crab still survives in the larger of the West Indian islands, though its final extinction is probably at hand." This anticipation is probably realised, or so careful a naturalist as Mr. Gosse would not have failed to have noticed it.

It appears that these crabs live not only in an orderly society in their retreats in the mountains, but regularly once a year march down to the sea-

* " History of the Maroons," i. ciii.

side in a body to spawn. In the months of April or May they come forth from the stumps of hollow trees, from clefts in rocks, and holes in the ground, and start on their journey. The procession sets forward with the regularity of an army under the guidance of an experienced commander. The line of march is directed with geometrical accuracy; no deviation is made whatever obstacles may intervene. It is said the crabs will scale the walls of a house rather than turn aside. If, however, the country be intersected by rivers, they are seen to wind along the course of the stream. The march is generally performed at night, but if rain falls during the day they do not fail to profit by the occasion. When after a fatiguing journey, and escaping a thousand dangers—for they are sometimes three months in reaching the shore—they prepare to cast their spawn. For this purpose, the crab has no sooner reached the shore than it eagerly goes to the water, in order that the waves may wash off the spawn. The eggs are hatched under the sand, and the old ones remain until the new-born have acquired sufficient strength for the journey, when the patriarchs lead the way to their former habitations, followed by the young. In August they begin to fatten and prepare for moulting, fitting up their burrows with dry leaves and other materials; they close the entrance and remain inactive until they get rid of the old shell and are provided with a new one. They are considered to be in greatest perfection for the table when they are moulting; and this may be the reason, as they are such remarkably sagacious animals, why they take such pains to shut their doors and conceal their abodes. This is the last edition of Crabbe's Tales!

Reptiles are numerous, but very few of them, I believe, are venomous. Lizards abound—pretty little harmless creatures—but insects are the pest of the island. They crawl on the ground or float in the air as densely as a tropical sun can quicken them into life. Mosquitoes annoyed me excessively; at night one cannot rest without preventive curtains; but they are so pertinacious in pursuit of their prey, that if they can possibly squeeze in they will. It gives me a shudder to hear the booming of their trumpet of defiance; and they appear to pay more attention to a new-comer than to *habitués*. It is impossible not to admire the wonderful ways of insects; a hornet's, wasp's, or ant's nest is an extraordinary effort of instinctive mechanism; but I cannot love the artists. Ants, cockroaches, sandflies, chigoes, spiders, and wasps swarm everywhere. The white or wood ants have great nests, sometimes on the ground, but more generally on trees; and it is best not to meddle with them. Against the domestic branch of the family, which frequents the abodes of man, every precaution must be taken. Clothes and boots must be kept in tin cases; leather portmanteaus and saddlery are favourite articles of consumption with them; as for food, it severely taxes the ingenuity of the housekeeper to preserve it, and the feet of safes are usually plunged in water.

Cockroaches infest habitations wherever situated, and are of larger size than their brother and sister nuisances in our country. Scorpions sting whenever they have a chance, and I hear of centipedes of three inches long. You know my aversion to spiders. I never happened to encounter one in Jamaica, but I am told they exist of disgustingly huge dimensions. It is a curious fact that the hero of the popular tales—the traditional stories, no doubt, derived from Africa, the motherplace of the slaves—which the negroes delight to listen to is a spider; a large, black, Annancy spider, supposed to be the personification of cunning and success, two qualities which have a special charm for the negro mind.* "They are called Ananzi stories," says Doctor Dasent,

* "Letters from Jamaica," p. 117.

"because so many of them turn on the feats of Ananzi, whose character is a mixture of the 'master-thief' and of 'Boots.' . . . In all the West Indian Islands 'Ananzi' is the name of spiders in general, and of a very beautiful species with yellow stripes in particular. The negroes think the cunning of this spider enables him to take any shape he pleases; in fact, he is the example which the African tribes—from which these stories came—have chosen to take as pointing out the superiority of wit over brute strength." And again: "The belief that men, under certain conditions, could take the shape of animals is primæval, and the traditions of every race can tell of such transformations."[*]

Specimens of some of these stories, "taken down from the lips of the narrators," are given in the little work, LETTERS FROM JAMAICA, to which I have before referred, and which I advise you to read.

Two habitations—nests would scarcely be a correct designation—of trap-door spiders are now before me. How wonderful are the provisions of nature! They were cut out of soft ground on a bank by the roadside. The cell is a cone, as like the bowl of a tobacco-pipe as possible, formed

---

[*] "Norse Tales," lxiii.

by a concretion of the soil. The inside is glazed and is as smooth as can be, with a circular cover fitting accurately, the top of the cavity (whence their name) opening and shutting with perfect regularity, a glutinous substance like silver paper being used for a hinge. The artificer is black, with short legs, and his bite is said to be venomous.

There is a curious insect which has been pointed out to me here—it might be mistaken for a little bit of dry stick—about two inches long. When it wishes to move it throws out two long legs on each side, and away it jumps. It is not mentioned by Gosse, I think.

The chigoe, or, as it is commonly called, the jigger, is a pleasant insect to keep company with. He penetrates the skin and burrows there. A cavity is formed by it, in which it constructs a bag, wherein it deposits its eggs and hatches a numerous family; and all this perhaps under one's big toe-nail. Negroes, being generally barefooted, are very subject to its perforations; but the British shoe and stocking are not proof against its ingress, and an officer has been laid up here for some weeks with an abscess under a toe-nail occasioned by the entrance of a jigger. Had he applied to a negro or negress, instead of to the medico, he would probably have been delivered of it at once. It is an operation requiring some delicate manipulation, but practice makes perfect. With a needle they widen the orifice, and work round the bag, which is about the size of a pea, so as to remove it unbroken. The danger lies in the fracture of the bag; then the progeny escapes into the wound, and ulceration will result. This, however, seldom occurs when the needle is in black hands, and the operation is performed without pain or loss of blood. Jiggers are rarely met with up here on the hills, but in the low country they are prevalent. I saw a dear little English boy suffering from one.

Notwithstanding these drawbacks, I maintain that existence in Jamaica is very enjoyable. I think that I cannot better finish my natural history than by quoting the quaint language of Sydney Smith, which is strongly corroborative of my assertion.

"Insects are the curse of tropical climates. Chigoes bury themselves in your flesh, and hatch a large colony of young chigoes in a few hours. Flies get entry into your mouth, into your eyes, into your nose; you eat flies, drink flies, and breathe flies. Lizards, cockroaches, and snakes get into your bed; ants eat up the books; scorpions sting you on the foot. Everything bites, stings, or bruises; every second of your life you are wounded by some piece of animal life. An insect with eleven legs is swimming in your tea-cup; a nondescript with nine wings is struggling in the small beer; or a caterpillar, with several dozen eyes in his belly, is hastening over the bread and butter. All nature is alive, and seems to be getting all her entomological host to eat you up as you are standing out of your coat, waistcoat, and breeches! Such are the tropics! All this reconciles us to our dens, bogs, vapours, and drizzle; to our apothecaries rushing about with gargle and tincture; to our old British constitutional coughs, sore throats, and swelled faces."*

June 23rd.—This is my farewell day at Newcastle. The mules have arrived to carry my luggage to the mail steamer's office at Kingston, with the exception of a small assortment which is to be sent on to Widcombe, together with that of some other guests here who are invited to pass the night there. The negro servants came out to see the last of me; one handmaiden was called Janetta, and the stout cook was Justina. Romantic names are now in vogue, and Sambos and Quashebas are nearly as defunct as are those of the overseers and drivers of the black cattle in those remarkably "good old days." Sambo, by

* *Edinburgh Review* for 1826, p. 310.

PLANTS, VEGETABLES, AND ANIMALS. 277

the way, is the name given to the offspring of a mulatto and a black; and the old names given to negroes in story-books were, in reality, neither promiscuously appropriated nor meaningless. They have a general signification, and have been used to indicate the day of the week on which the individual was born—a custom which probably dates from their arrival in a Christian land. An infant born on a Sunday, for instance, if a male, would be named Quashie, if a female, Quasheba; the affix "ba" appearing to be the mark of the feminine gender.

	Male.	Female.
Sunday	*Quashie*, cunning	*Quasheba*, slender.
Monday	*Cudjoe*, strong-headed	*Juba*, clever.
Tuesday	*Cubbina*, inventive	*Beneba*, handsome.
Wednesday	*Quaco*, bad luck	*Cooba*, stout.
Thursday	*Quao*, ugly	*Abba*, strong physic.
Friday	*Cuffie*, hot-tempered	*Fibba*, gentle.
Saturday	*Quamin*, full of tricks	*Mimba*, wild.

In like manner the children born in Pitcairn's Island, the issue of the mutineers of the *Bounty*, are denominated with the addition of the month, as "Thursday October Christian." As I am on *domestic* matters, perhaps it will interest you to know the prices of a few items. Mutton is 1s. per lb., Beef 6d.; 1½d. to the "service" for rations; a chicken 1s. 6d. to 2s. Butter is the dearest article,

2s. 6d. per lb. It is imported in tins, chiefly from America and Ireland. No butter is made for sale about here; I should doubt if it be even in the agricultural districts of the island, certainly not to any extent, or the imported butter would not be used at that price.*

I mounted Beethoven, and rode to join Mr. and Mrs. M——, who are also going to Widcombe. We rode by the barracks, and past the recreation-room. *En passant*, I may remark that it is to be regretted that there is no bath made for the men. I am told that it has been repeatedly recommended by commanding officers in their reports, without any notice being taken of the suggestion. There is a dell just below the barracks admirably adapted for the purpose, into which a mountain spring discharges itself. A very small outlay would convert this into a plunging-bath. I am sure that it would be good policy and economy; it would improve the health of the garrison, physically and morally. Cleanliness and amusement are important hygienic principles. A soldier's life is a dull one here; beyond the regimental recreation-room there is not a resource

---

* As to expensive articles, what do you think of a pair of donkeys being sold for £750! I am confidently informed such was the case lately: they were "Poitou Jacks"—enormous animals.

except a fives-court, and this is not quite the climate for that exercise. The men do not, as a rule, care for a simple constitutional; in fact they have walking enough, and many of them earn extra pay by employment in the engineer's department. There are plots of ground allotted to the soldiers for gardens, and there is entomological amusement in the shape of catching butterflies and other insects; but few men have taste for these pursuits. As the consequence of no resource in off-duty hours they take to drinking, and fevers or other maladies, or perhaps deaths, ensue. I don't suppose that a bath would prove a panacea, but it would refresh and invigorate the heated body.

The heat is great to-day, and of course as we descend the hill the more oppressive it becomes. We diverged from our straight course in order to pay our respects to Commodore and Mrs. De Horsey at their private residence. They were, however, at Port Royal. As we rode along a largish snake scuttled away among the bushes by the roadside. For the last two miles we cantered through woods. I noticed several calabash trees; they are about the height and dimension of our apple-trees, with crooked lateral branches; the fruit is enclosed in a shell, which is the calabash of which one has often heard, and which serves the natives for drinking-cups and other domestic purposes. They are susceptible of being polished and engraved. I procured one thus prepared and lined with silk, intended to do duty as a lady's work-bag.

We reached the hospitable mansion of Colonel C—— at luncheon time. Shall I ever forget the luxurious rest which I enjoyed when I was shown afterwards to the apartment which was prepared for me in a little villa detached from the house?— open at both ends with jalousies, so that it was deliciously fresh. Having taken down a volume of Dickens from the book-shelves, I threw myself on a comfortable sofa, with brandy and seltzer by my side, and a cigar in my mouth. The heat and the ride had induced a state of dreamy languor, so that the *dolce far niente* was exceedingly agreeable. In the evening several guests arrived, some to pass the night, others to ride back again. B—— and F——, some neighbouring clergymen and their wives, some officers from Up-park Camp, a naval officer lately arrived, and Captain and Mrs. M——, who were to be shipmates with me on board the homeward-bound *Nile*. There is a feeling of independence in getting about on horseback, and the ladies, with a riding-skirt over their evening dress, manage to enter the drawing-room with quite an unruffled appearance.

I passed a very pleasant evening, and after the out-lying guests had ridden away, and the ladies at home had retired, some of us sat out on the terrace enjoying the delightful coolness of the night, until small hours compelled us to "turn-in," although in this climate one never wants to go to bed.

Wednesday, June 24.—I slept well, notwithstanding that I was aroused by the screams of a peacock, the habitual roost of which, I had been informed, was on the ridge of the shingled roof of my villa. Oftentimes in his sleep he loses his balance and rolls down the declivity. However, I slept on again, till I was awoke by some one at my bedside. "Marnin, sar," I exclaimed; "how did you sleep?" thinking it was B——, who occupied the adjoining room; but on drawing aside the mosquito curtains I found it was the attentive black butler, who, somewhat surprised at my salutation, had brought the early tea. He informed me that there was a spring not far off in the woods where I could bathe; so I arose and proceeded thither, and found others bent on the same errand.

At 8.30 all the household, black and white, was assembled for family prayer, and I never saw a more attentive congregation. After breakfast I took leave of my kind entertainers, and B——, F——, and I drove off in a buggy to Kingston. Two miles from Kingston is the chief military station, Up-park Camp; then there is a race-course, and you come to the suburban villas and pinguin fences of which I have already spoken, and then you enter the streets of Kingston. Considering the important position it has held for so long a time, having been the commercial capital ever since the reduction of Port Royal, it is singularly plain and dingy. An appearance of gloom and heaviness strikes the visitor at once. There is no amusement in the place; there is a theatre, the only one in the island, but it is seldom open. It is lighted with cocoanut oil lamps, for as yet, as I have previously recorded, Jamaica is innocent of gas.

The population numbers about 50,000, all employed in business, for no one lives in Kingston for pleasure. There must be great want of public spirit here; otherwise, why should a population, amidst which considerable wealth must be scattered, be without gas, when it is dark at sunset, and a small island like St Thomas's is already provided with it. The town is bountifully supplied with excellent water, which is brought in through pipes from the Hope River, a distance of several miles, and yet the streets are always dirty; and, although fires are frequent, there is no fire brigade, nor does advantage seem to have been taken to rebuild demolished houses with modern improvements. Kingston was constituted a corporate town in 1801, it is a parish in itself, and is governed by a custos of its own, who is, I suppose, an irresponsible officer, with no one to look after him—

"Quis custodiet ipsos custodes"?

I have before stated that all the streets cut one another at right angles; those that run north and south commence at the harbour, so that one end of them is sea and the other country. At the top of three of these streets is the grand square or parade, with a statue of Lord Metcalfe. At the end of King Street, one of the cross streets and the best street, the statue of Lord Rodney, removed from Spanish Town, has been set up.

There are churches, chapels, and conventicles for all religious denominations in abundance. They, however, do not add to the liveliness of the place, although I hope to its sanctity; but from what I heard, Kingston is "no better than it should be." We are passing St. Andrew's, which was the parish church; and it may or may not please the members of the Liberation Society to hear that, notwithstanding disestablishment, the Church of England is flourishing here. It is a brick edifice with a spire, remarkable for nothing except its ugliness (which may be said of all the churches I saw in Jamaica), and the monumental slab placed over the remains of the gallant Benbow. A local poet was inspired on the occasion, and wrote—

> "The Kingston town folk with sorrow did go
> To see the last of brave old Benbow."

He was not "old," however, only fifty-two. The slab lies within the communion-rails, and has his coat of arms incised, with this inscription :—

"Here lyeth interred the body of John Benbow, Esq., Admiral of the White. A true pattern of English courage. Who lost his life in defence of his Queen and Country, November ye 4th, 1702, in the 52nd year of his age, by a wound in his leg received in an engagement with Mons. Du Casse. Being much lamented."

Public carriages, mostly of the "buggy" style, called busses, ply about the streets, the fare being 6*d.* per person *par course.* The hotels, I hear, are not first-rate, dignified by the name of halls, the best being Blundel Hall, kept by Louisa Grant, a sister of the eminent Mother Seacoal of Crimean fame.

There are several newspapers in the colony. I do not know how many are published at Kingston, but Gall's *Telegraphic News Letter* emanates from this locality, and is a handy little octavo sheet, issued three times a week, at the moderate charge of 12s. per annum "when paid in advance." It contains the latest intelligence per wire or steamer, advertisements, and local news.

The advertisements are sometimes diverting, for instance :—

"GLORIOUS TOBACCO.—Where on earth did you get this? Why, man, it puts a soul into me and I feel as if I could dream of nothing but what is beautiful. By Jove—that's the Tobacco for a man to buy. Let's see the label. 'Fine Cut Cavendish, from the finest plantations in the State of Virginia, only to be had in Jamaica from C. E. BRUCK, Harbour Street, Kingston.'—April 1, 1874."

When the editor indulges in a "leader," it will be perceived that his pen may be dipped in that essence which is a synonym of his name. Here is a specimen of the odium theologicum :—

"Thursday, May 28, 1874.—What folly will not the Jamaica Church be guilty of? The Tomfoolery seems to be contagious, for we find Mr. J. G. Harris, of Mavis Bank, figuring in the columns of the 'Semi-Weekly Gleaner' upon the very important item of information, that the 'Priest of Mavis Bank,' not finding a dressmaker in Jamaica capable of cutting and doing up a surplice of the most approved pattern, has actually imported one from England by the Royal Mail Steamer, while the short-sighted and ignorant Custom-house officers, failing to see the grave necessity for such importation of enlightenment and intelligence, actually charged 5s. duty because they could not discriminate between a bottle of mixed pickles and a genuine 'ritualistic surplice.' Alas! alas! What are we coming to when matters of the kind can fill a column of our local paper, never to speak of the valuable waste of time to Mr. Harris in penning it! It is true that our pen may be dipped in Gall, but we think that makes a better.

ink than the waste vinegar from an empty bottle of mixed pickles. Poor Mr. Harris! His time can't be worth much. And alas for the Mavis Bank pulpit when it requires a ritualistic surplice by packet for the declaration of Christian truth therefrom! The columns of the 'Gleaner' seem to be easily filled."

Here is some parochial news :—

"PAROCHIAL NEWS.—St. James, March 9.—Much dissatisfaction prevails in the parish about the post, its arrival is so uncertain as to time. Samwell & Co., with their equestrians and animals, performed two nights last week to a very full tent. The 'piece de resistance' at this circus was the goat riding, but altogether the performance excited the admiration of a large audience. There is no lack of variety in the entertainment, for besides the equestrians, there were dogs, monkeys, &c., giving proof of savage education. The District Court sat during the week, and the conviction of a boy for stealing yams caused such grief to the mother that she threw herself down and cut her forehead on the stone steps, then she set up a cry and went through the market-square yelling like a maniac. The Board of Health met, and made arrangements to the effect, that in case small-pox should come into the town the District Prison be used as a hospital. The child reported before to have had the disease is now said to have only had chicken pox. The weather is extremely dry, and strong breezes blowing; grass is very much burnt. Sugar-making has been going on rapidly. The ginger crop is now said to be small, as much of the plants have been found rotting on the ground. Mr. Sergeant Simon, the member elected for Dewsbury, is a native of this parish; he practiced as a barrister in the island for a short time after being called to the bar."

The "meeting of the Board of Health," to make arrangements *in case* small-pox should come into the town, and the child reported to have the disease and afterwards stated to be suffering only from chicken-pox, would leave the impression that, if the contradiction of the report were true, there was not a case of small-pox in Kingston. I hope I am not incorrectly maligning the town, when I express my belief that it is never without more or less small-pox. In this instance, it is to be feared that "the child" had something more serious than "chicken-pox," for not long afterwards the following announcement appeared :—

"Passengers by the Steamers from this port to St. Thomas, in consequence of the prevalence of small-pox here, will be required to give a guarantee that they will pay the expense of eleven days' quarantine in the Lazaretto at St. Thomas, at £1 per day."

I cannot resist giving you one more cutting, and then I have done with the Jamaica press : —

"Clothing . . ready-made . . Ready for putting on,
  To go to Church
  To go to a Wedding
  To go to a Christening
  To go to a Funeral
  To go to the Theatre
  To call on the Governor
  To pay a visit
   AT WILLIAM MALABRE & CO'S,
  Corner of King and Harbour Streets, Kingston,
Where every man, woman, and child now goes for an outfit, because they meet the requirements of the age, and for quality and workmanship, they are not to be equalled in Jamaica.
   A full suit of Black, for 40s.
   A strong and well made Sack for 4s.
   A better article for 5s.
   A woolen Shirt for 6s.

> A print Shirt, from 3s to 4s.
> A pair of Ancle Boots for 4s 3d.
> A pair of Elastic side Boots, from 8s to 10s.
> Felt Hats, from 3s 6d to 6s.
> Hurrah! Jessie!!
> I'm off to Malabre's."

I visited the stores of the Cuban Count Duany, to lay in a stock of "Creole" cigars for the voyage. This term is applied not only to persons but to the productions of the island. These cigars are extensively used at the messes, and they are certainly very good, considerably cheaper than Havannas, but not so fine in aroma as those of the best brands manufactured in Cuba; but I presume the quality of those grown here will be improved in time. The *Colonial Standard* (a local paper), of the 13th July, 1873, thus describes them:—

"We have to congratulate Count Duany on the eminent success which has attended his tobacco plantations at Hall Head Estate, in St. Thomas in the East. Only a year or two ago this fine estate fell into the hands of the Count, who at once perceived the adaptability of the soil for tobacco, and determined to establish that staple there, to go hand in hand with sugar and rum. The year's crop has realised over three hundred bales of the finest quality tobacco, grown from imported reed.

We believe this is the largest crop that has been as yet produced in any single plantation in Jamaica."

A matter that deserves to be chronicled is the profound tranquillity which the island enjoys at present. A military force not exceeding 900 men, and a police of 680, controlling a population of upwards of half a million, is a convincing proof of the harmless nature of the Creoles, and of the content which pervades all classes. When we cast our eyes around at the condition of Cuba and Hispaniola, distant only a steamer's one day's voyage, we may congratulate ourselves on the wisdom of British rule. In no part of the world can travelling be accomplished with greater personal security than in Jamaica. Ladies and gentlemen ride home at night from entertainments, and I never heard of any one taking the precaution of being armed. In private houses—so far as I know—doors and windows are left unfastened by day and by night. Larcenies were pretty frequent, especially during the last year of the failure of the crops, when provisions were dear; but, in the words of the Governor's Report (p. 57.), "It is very seldom, in Jamaica, that in cases of burglary violence is used to effect an entrance. This is a curious characteristic of the criminal classes here. In the vast majority of instances the thief gets into the house by a door or corridor, which has either been carelessly fastened or left wide open. Out of fifty-one of these offences in Kingston, only four were effected by violent entrance. It is an equally curious characteristic of the non-criminal classes here, that the knowledge of this peculiar habit of the burglars has so little effect upon storekeepers and other householders in inducing them to take proper care of their property. The number of shops and other houses in Kingston, discovered by the constabulary during the year to have been left open at night, was 199. And there is, probably, much less of this carelessness in Kingston than in other places. In the town of Falmouth, the constabulary found, during the year, no less than fifty doors and windows unfastened."

By the courtesy of the Commodore in charge at Jamaica, a steam-launch was sent to convey us to Port Royal. The naval command here used to be held by an admiral, and the military by a general, but in these days of economical administration these positions are supplied by a post-captain and a colonel. We embarked at the Ordnance-yard, and in about three-quarters of an hour we found ourselves abreast of the old *Aboukir*, the guard-ship. Several other men-of-war happened to be there. We went on board the *Eclipse*, a fine steam-sloop, as one of our party wished to see her captain. The *Wye* was just getting under weigh. We landed at the Dock-yard. The Admiralty House is a spacious one, with wide passages and plenty of doors and windows, and therefore can be kept cool—very necessary in this nook of land, where the sun always shines with unmitigated power. The windows being kept open before and behind, a moderate gale was blowing through the drawing-room, while the jalousies entirely excluded the solar rays.

A kind reception awaited us. We saw the portrait of Lord Rodney by "Sir Joshua," and also full-lengths of George III. and his Queen, which are the property of the Government of Jamaica. Artists always do the best for their sitters, certainly for a queen; but Charlotte of Mecklenberg-Strelitz must have been as unpromising a subject as they ever had to deal with; her hands and arms, however, were beautiful.

Port Royal, as I have previously stated, is situated on the point of a narrow neck of land, which, projecting nearly nine miles from the main line of coast, forms the southern barrier of the harbour. This narrow strip is called "The Palisades," a very old name, the derivation of which a remark of Sloane's probably gives us: "the sand kept up by palisadoes." * I have also mentioned how Port Royal has been curtailed in its dimensions, and shorn of its wealth and importance by earthquakes, hurricanes, and ravages of the sea. The whole aspect of the place is arid, blighted, and melancholy. It is very hot, and affords no refuge from the sun. There is a large Naval Hospital, a fine building. Port Royal possesses a solitary advantage—it is healthy at present; the inmates of the hospital are therefore few, but a staff of three medical officers is maintained to operate upon about as many patients. One hundred beds can be made up, or more upon an emergency. We walked through the Barrack Square; the ground is gravelled over, but I am told that the sea percolates through the sandy sub-soil, and the salt oozes out on the surface. The barracks are at present occupied only by a detachment of artillery and a company of the 2nd W. I. Regiment. There is only one artillery officer. A dull life for him, perhaps you will remark. Yes; but he can mess every

* "Voyages," p. lix.

PLANTS, VEGETABLES, AND ANIMALS. 293

day on board the *Aboukir*, where there is a good table kept, and generally well-attended by visitors from other men-of-war which happen to be at the station. The gunners were playing at cricket on this bad ground: how innate is the British love of athletic games. But this appears to be the only possible shore recreation of the garrison, for there is not a walk except along the sandy palisades; but they can indulge in bathing, boating, and fishing. These pursuits are not altogether unattended by risk, on account of the numerous sharks and coral reefs.

Port Royal, as a place of defence, is of great importance. Ships, in advancing towards the harbour, must necessarily pass between shoals and rocks, through a difficult passage, in some parts extremely narrow, and would be inevitably exposed to a destructive fire from the guns of Port Royal, and from the opposite side they would be raked by the battery of the "Twelve Apostles." Should they be enabled to pass these, they would still have to encounter the guns of Fort Augusta, a formidable position, commanding the whole range of the harbour. So that doubtless, if a landing were contemplated, it would not be made here, but on some of the many unprotected harbours elsewhere on the coast, as would be the case with us in England; our fortified seaports would be avoided. This is always supposing that there were guns for these purposes; but at present all those in position would be perfectly harmless against ironclads; and I have since heard that the guns at Fort Augusta have been dismounted and sold, and the officer who was employed in this work informed me that among them were several undoubted Spanish guns, the metal of which they were composed being generally superior to the rest. Some of these might well have been retained and sent to the Artillery Museum at Woolwich, where there are no specimens of Spanish guns of their date.

The officers' quarters are very fair, large, and airy rooms; we were hospitably received and entertained there by the solitary officer, who regaled us with iced Moselle cup. In this climate it is surprising with what impunity one can drink; the throat so soon becomes parched, that one really feels the want of liquids. We had just partaken of tea at the Admiralty House, and now we were quite ready for this fresh libation.

I amused myself by turning over the leaves of an old Royal Artillery mess account-book. The dates ranged from 1827 to 1835, and I was astounded at the prodigious amount of liquors consumed in those good old days. The accounts are not kept with much accuracy; perhaps the hands that wrote were somewhat shaky. As far as we could make out, the number of dining members must have been five or six, although the accounts show a much smaller number, not giving the names of those who paid their bills regularly.

The usual monthly consumption was 160 bottles of Madeira, 24 claret, 30 brandy, besides ale and porter. Champagne, port, and sherry were but rarely drunk. The consumption was frequently far greater; the number of dining members probably fluctuating from three to seven or thereabouts.

What "Nights at Mess!" The chaplain was evidently the jolliest of the party; his bill for one month was £56 5s. 9d.; that of the only other dining member recorded being £20 7s. 5d. His name first appears in the account for March, 1827, and then it disappears; but in February, 1835, his name is recorded as being present, so that hard drinking does not seem to have disagreed with him.

Mr. D—— kindly offered to write out for me the expenditure of liquor during the eight years.

I have now received it, and I think it worth preserving, so I present it *in extenso*:—

STATEMENT OF CELLAR.

JANUARY, 1830.	Madeira.	Champ.	Claret.	Porter.	Ale.	Port.	Sherry.	Brandy.
Remaining in Cellar Jan. 1	619	6	30	—	40	—	22	145
Received into Cellar . . .	—	6	—	100	12	12	—	—
	619	12	30	100	52	12	22	145
Expended from Jan. 1 to 23	329	9	19	64	49	9	—	63
Remaining in Cellar Jan. 23	290	3	11	36	3	3	22	82

(This was the largest expenditure during the eight years.)

Extract showing the consumption of Madeira and brandy during the period:—

	Madeira.	Brandy.
1827. June	157	9
„ October . . .	219	7
„ December . . .	377	10
1828. January . . .	285	—
„ May	185	—
„ September . .	163	23
1829. January . . .	171	24
„ July	212	21
„ December . . .	207	45
1830. August . . .	183	16
„ December . .	168	22
1831. January . . .	200	22½
„ October . . .	192	5½
1832. April . . .	130	11½
„ December . . .	156	43
1833. January . . .	203	35
„ March . . .	125	34½
.„ December . . .	221¼	28

PLANTS, VEGETABLES, AND ANIMALS.

	Madeira.	Brandy.
1834. March	216	28
,, July	$198\frac{1}{4}$	59
,, December	301	33
1835. February	237	—

These are curious details. Fortunately, these "merry days" are past; but it is self-evident that where there are no other resources, men are driven to find their pleasure in hard drinking, and to drown their ennui "in the bowl."

There were, formerly, two forts here, called Fort Charles and Fort James, erected in the early days of British possession, when Charles II. had mounted the throne. The former of the two is built of bricks, which, I suppose, were brought from England. A dial-stone, "aged and worn," is fixed on a wall, the last figures of a date .. 70 only remain, no doubt 1670. The latter fort is very much *in statu quo*, but its brother was submerged by the earthquake, and has now six or seven fathoms of water over it. Its resting-place is marked by a buoy, sometimes erroneously called the "Church buoy," being supposed to be moored over the sunken church; but that structure, being less firmly built, is said to have fallen into pieces.

Then we walked out, through some miserable streets, broken-down tenements, the inhabitants looking as dilapidated as their houses. Squalid children, but with distended stomachs, quite naked, were playing in the dirt. The names of some of the streets are posted up at the corners: "New Street"—not a misnomer probably at the time of the British conquest; a "Broad Street" of not many score yards in length, the rest, doubtless,

"In the deep bosom of the ocean buried;"

and "Cannon Street," one of the largest. The present population of this "City of the Sea" numbers nearly fifteen hundred. Then we procured the keys of the church, and entered. Like the rest of her sisters, it can boast of no beauty, either inside or out. It is built of brick, in the shape of a cross, and dates from 1760, I think. The only handsome piece of work about it is the organ and loft, which are of fine mahogany. The walls are covered with mortuary tablets; and almost all, with scarcely any exception, record the same cause of death—that contagion which has hurried so many of England's gallant sons to untimely graves. As you pass from one to another, you read, "died of yellow fever," "died of yellow fever." Sad but salutary warnings to the congregation are these short "sermons in stones."

One tablet I thought especially touching:—

> Sacred to the Memory
> of
> HENRY CARR, aged 13, EDWARD RICE, aged 16,
> JAMES TALLEN, aged 16,
> Midshipmen H. M. S. *Sapphire*, who died
> of yellow fever, at Port Royal, June 1820.
> This stone is erected as a tribute of affection
> by their Captain.

What mothers' tears were shed when those poor boys embarked for the West Indies, and how bitterly renewed again so shortly after! Often the death of a marine is recorded on the same tablet with the officers—doubtless the servant who attended them faithfully to the last.

At six o'clock the launch was again in readiness for us at the Dock-yard stairs. There was some wind now, and consequently more "sea on," and it was frequently *on* our backs and *on* our faces, and everywhere with some tossing, which the ladies did not enjoy. In an hour's time we were landed at the Ordnance-yard, and from it we made our way on board the *Nile*, which had arrived the day before from Colon, and was now coaling for her homeward voyage. Captain Revett and his officers seemed quite pleased to see me again; it was like meeting old friends, and I felt quite at home. We enjoyed a cold dinner in the saloon, and afterwards repaired to the Captain's cabin on deck, where we sat and talked till it was time to say good-bye. Mrs. C—— had been so kind and useful: she had accompanied us all day. B—— and little F—— and I exchanged affectionate farewells. Thus ends my visit to Jamaica, and highly I have enjoyed it. The health and strength I have gained are not among the least of its advantages.

Captain M——, whom I had met at Mrs. C——'s, was on board with his wife. He and I sat talking on deck, but the dust from the coaling was disagreeable; and although the night was very hot, I before long retired to my berth, for we had had a long day's work.

CHAPTER XV.

COALING.—CLOSE SHAVING.—HOMEWARD BOUND.

Thursday, June 25th.—A very disturbed night, what with heat, mosquitoes, and the noise, for coaling never ceased till 8 o'clock this morning, when 570 tons had been taken on board. I had to go ashore in search of my luggage, which had not arrived. I found it at the agent's, who should have forwarded it. I also went to the Victoria Market, for Messrs. Alberga had recommended a salesman, who was to supply me with pines, some avocado pears, and a few sweet potatoes, packed for the voyage. By-the-bye, I saw at Widcombe a "life" plant, as it was called; so vivacious is it, that a leaf placed anywhere will grow, not requiring water or any care. A leaf, with a nail through it to fasten it to a wall, will thrive and grow and put forth leaves. I am bringing a sprig home. When again on board I asked for a barber: the Captain said I should have one directly.

The operator was evidently close at hand, and quickly presented himself at my cabin—a white man who had never left Kingston—and he tried to make himself as pleasant as members of his profession generally think to be part of their business. I like to be quiet while under manipulation; certainly while being shaved it is dangerous to reply. He shaved me, cut my hair, and sprinkled Florida water over my head. I inquired how much to pay. "Four shillings." "Well," I said, "that's moderate." He pretended not to understand my tone, and expressed himself gratified to have given me satisfaction. I replied that I found no fault with his performance, only with his charge. "It's the time that it takes." "Well," I answered, "shaving does not take long, or ought not, and I have not much hair to cut. So there's a florin, and I consider you are well paid." He took it and thanked me; evidently it was only a "try on."

I find that there are a good many passengers on board, amongst them our Minister at Lima, with his pretty Peruvian wife. I had heard much of the beauty of her countrywomen, and when I saw this lady I was not disappointed. We have also embarked the late Colonial Secretary of Jamaica, with his wife and daughter, besides many residents; so, at all events, there will be plenty of agreeable companions for the voyage.

We got under weigh about 10 A.M. The engines were stopped off Port Royal, and a man-of-war's boat, under charge of an officer, came alongside, and a bag of letters was handed up. The screw again revolves, we pass through the narrow passage, double the promontory, and are out in the open sea; but there was no more motion than in the harbour.

Friday, the 26*th.*—We are off Jacmel. The Captain said that we should not be allowed to land, so I declined a seat in the mail-boat. We are in quarantine on account of small-pox at Jamaica. I am sorry now that I took a return ticket, and that I did not return by Cuba and the United States, which would not have consumed much more time; for now I shall see nothing but what I have seen before, indeed, rather less, as we are prohibited from landing. I had a good deal of conversation with Mr. Jerningham, I know so many of his relations and friends. He is a tall, distinguished-looking man; he is coming home for his health; he appears to be suffering a good deal.

Sunday, the 28*th.*—Entered the harbour of St. Thomas. The health-officer came off to us, and informed us from his galley that we were in quarantine; so the yellow flag is flying at our fore, and a police-boat rows round us to prevent communication. The toy-town looked so bright and gay, for all the numerous public and private flagstaffs have their colours displayed, and the Dannebrog flies over the Government House and Fort. Charlotte Amalia is the proper name of the town, but every one knows it only as St. Thomas's. Masses of scarlet berries growing along the water's edge form a charming border to the town. There was a question raised as to what they were; some of us thought them "Flamboyants," but a Jamaica gentleman pronounced them to be Barbadoes' pride (*Ponciana pulcherrima*).

A boat-load of poultry and vegetables for our use is being hauled in, and about fifty new passengers, nearly all Spanish-speaking people, but a very plain lot, are gradually appearing with their chairs on deck. If we receive as many at Barbadoes, I tremble for my cabin. At present I occupy the same one as on the former voyage, calculated for four persons. I cannot expect to retain that if we are crowded; all I stipulate for is one to myself, however small. I dislike the idea of sharing it with others. We are coaling again. I thought that work had been completed at Jamaica. A huge barge is alongside, and I watch the operation from my cabin window. I perceive that the women do the hardest work, carrying the coals; the negro lords of creation fill the baskets, and thus rest between whiles. How these women do labour! The heat is very oppressive, and I laid myself down on my sofa and fell asleep, and when I awoke after two hours' sleep, there they were at work still, laughing all the same. How different our lots are! You are passing a quiet Sunday at home; fancy what a day of noise, confusion, and dust I have had. The coaling is almost finished, and it was the noise of weighing the anchor that awoke me. The steam crane has been screaming all day, but the grating noise of the chain cable passing through the hawse-hole beats everything that is disagreeable. It sets one's teeth on edge.

Tuesday, the 30*th.*—We are running along the shore of Barbadoes. The island is in the shape of a leg of mutton, twenty-eight miles long and twenty-four broad, tapering down to three. It is flat; one can look miles over its green expanse, plentifully dotted with small towns or villages, churches, villas, and *usines.* Were it not for the characteristic palms, there would be nothing tropical about it in appearance; it might be a bit of England. It is thickly populated, about 162,000 in all, of which there are about 17,000 whites.

At 2 P.M. we brought up in Carlisle Bay. The Captain said he should try hard to get us on shore. He and I were invited by Mr. C——, our outward-bound passenger, to dine with him on our return. The inevitable health-officer came off directly to us. "Clean bills of health?" "No." "Then you are in quarantine." Up went the yellow flag, and the water-police boat, with a talkative crew of negroes, kept guard upon us. The Captain requested the health-officer to send a letter to the Governor, in which he represented that we were all healthy on board, and that there was no more small-pox at Jamaica than there was usually; whereupon, in due course of time, the good-natured Governor gave us *pratique*. It was now the dinner-hour on board, and I thought I had better take the precaution of dining before I started for the shore. So, after a hearty meal, Captain M—— and two other fellow-passengers and I jumped into a shore-boat. The Captain declined to accompany us, his avocations preventing him. A crowd of negroes on the quay were anxious to be of service to us.

We made our way to the club; I asked for Mr. C——. "He is gone to Trinidad to-day." A gentleman standing by came forward, and introducing himself as Mr. O'N——, said he was his partner, and would be happy to do anything for us. I said Mr. C—— had invited Captain Revett and me to dine with him on our return voyage. Mr. O'N—— said that the ordinary telegram had announced that the *Nile* had embarked no passengers at Jamaica, so Mr. C—— thought I should arrive by the next mail; and, having business at Trinidad, he took advantage of a steamer, and must have passed under the bows of the *Nile* as we entered the harbour. Mr. O'N—— insisted in standing in the place of Mr. C ——, and invited us all to dine at the club or at his private residence. As I mentioned that we had already dined, he took us into the club, and gave us a most refreshing Barbadian beverage called "Falernan," and we hurried off, as Captain M—— wished to call upon the General; so we got into a carriage, promising Mr. O'N—— that we would return to the club. A few minutes' drive brought us to the gates of the General's residence. We sat some time talking in his drawing-room, which by the way had a carpet, the first I have seen since I left England.

General M—— is a great botanist, and has a renowned garden, but unfortunately it was too dark to see it; and I fear, as it was, we encroached upon his dinner-hour. We took our leave, and then drove to the barracks, as I wished to see H—— S—— of the 98th. As I stood in the corridor, I saw the officers at mess. H—— came out as soon as he received my card. How little I expected, when I saw him last in London, that our next meeting would be in a West Indian island. He pressed me to come into the mess-room, but my light suit was not adapted for evening dress, even if time had admitted. So I looked at his room, a fine large airy one, and hurried down to my companions. These are fine barracks; the next block is occupied by the West Indian regiment. It seems a pity to have reduced the number of these useful regiments, so valuable in tropical climates. What good service the 2nd West did on the Gold Coast! There were twelve of these black regiments kept on foot till 1801, when six were disbanded. Four of these were reduced in 1870.

To drive about in the dark to see the place appeared somewhat ridiculous, so we went back to the club. Mr. O'N—— had been home and dined, and now he was in readiness to receive

us. He introduced us to some other gentlemen,
and we had much cheerful conversation, so that
with excellent cigars and delectable potations
we were sorry to move. I was glad to hear that
the sugar crop was likely to be the best ever
produced there, abundance of rain having fallen,
which is the important element of success. I also
learnt that petroleum is being exported to a small
extent, the production of which in the clay formation of the part of the island called Scotland
is being developed.* Mr. O'N—— offered his services to show us the way to the quay. The streets
in Bridgetown are narrow; the principal one is
called Broad Street. Some fine public buildings
have just been completed at a cost of £26,000;
they are constructed of the limestone of the
island. The design seemed to me of the heavy
massive style; the moon was shining brightly
upon them, and we probably saw them in the most
favourable light. There is also on the *Grande Place*

---

* In the Blue Book of 1872, the Governor, Mr. Rawson, calls
attention to the fact that the Moravians insist more upon the instruction
of the children in their congregations than the other religious denominations in the island, as the following table will show :—

	Number.	Scholars.	Proportion of scholars to population.
Church of England	144,080	12,370	9 per cent
Moravians	4,733	1,571	33 ,,
Wesleyans	12,267	2,408	19 ,,

a bronze statue of Lord Nelson, whose memory, and that of Lord Rodney, is still cherished by West Indians as having saved their island homes from war and desolation. A canal winds round the town and at its mouth forms a small dock; but my fellow-passengers were getting fidgety to regain the *Nile*, so we hailed a boat and pushed off. After heartily thanking Mr. O'N—— for his kind entertainment of us, we bade adieu to the hospitable shores of the little island, which I hear is called the " Paris of the West Indies."

On our return we found the decks crowded by an accession of passengers. Bayly came and said that he regretted having had to shift my effects from my cabin, which was already occupied by four ladies; but that the Captain had given up his cabin in the saloon to me, for which I felt grateful. It was a lovely night, and many of us remained on deck till the last lights of Barbadoes had faded from our sight; and thus I take probably my final leave of the West Indies.

> " Beautiful islands! where the green
> Which nature wears was never seen
> 'Neath zone of Europe ; where the hue
> Of sea and heaven is such a blue
> As England dreams not; where the night
> Is all irradiate with the light
> Of stars like moons, which, hung on high,

Breathe and quiver in the sky,
Each its silver haze divine
Flinging in a radiant line,
O'er gorgeous flower and mighty tree
On the soft and shadowy sea!
Beautiful islands! brief the time
I dwelt beneath your awful clime;
Yet oft I see in noon-day dream
Your glorious stars with lunar beam;
And oft before my sight arise
Your sky-like seas, your sea-like skies;
Your green bananas' giant leaves;
Your golden canes in arrowy sheaves;
Your palms which never die, but stand
Immortal sea-marks on the strand,—
Their feathery tufts, like plumage rare;
Their stems so high, so strange and fair!
Yea! while the breeze of England now
Flings rose-scents on my aching brow,
I think a moment I inhale
Again the breath of tropic gale."

CHAPTER XVI.

AT SEA.—AT HOME.

July 3rd.—I have omitted the record of some days, because nothing worth noting has occurred. We are a merry party on board, and are getting on easy terms with each other, but we have too many passengers for comfort. There is quite a labyrinth of chairs on deck, so that it is difficult to thread one's way in the daily "constitutionals." There is also a score of Spanish children who are always in the way, and some who are continually squalling. I believe that Spanish children surpass all others in this respect. I suppose it is considered a healthy expansion of their lungs, for I looked down the opening to the lower deck on one that had been in full cry for an hour; its parents and friends were quietly chatting around, not taking the slightest heed of it nor trying to quiet it.

The chief steward, Wilkinson, who is a very obliging person, told me he feared something had gone wrong with my pines. So I descended with him to the ice-house, the pines were taken out of the basket, and out of the twenty-four twelve were condemned at once to be thrown overboard; and as the remainder would not keep long, he offered to make use of them at the saloon tables instead of his own—which were in a better state of preservation—and give me the same number of fresh ones from his own stores when I left, which I thought very liberal on his part. An honest fellow, that salesman at Kingston! We are growing rather tired of pine-apples; we have them every day at dessert. One of us humorously remarks that the dullest part of the dinner is when we come to the *wine* and *pine*.

Eating goes on pretty nearly all day in the saloon, and the waiters have a hard time of it. They are obliged to double the number of the meals, as there are too many passengers to be seated at once; so that my cabin in the saloon is not so pleasant a situation as where I was before. The effect of eating on the ear and nostrils is incessant. As for the baths, they are in such demand, that I believe if you got up before daylight you would find somebody inside, and another waiting outside. I got up at 5 A.M. this morning, hoping to get first turn, and, lo! at the port-side bath-room door there was a passenger with his towel thrown over his shoulder, patiently sitting on a camp-stool. On the starboard-side one I just got in as another turned out. It is a recognised custom for the bather in possession to turn off the water and let in fresh whilst he is dressing. The ladies have baths on the lower deck. You must now be so well informed as to the life on board, that I need not specify the small events that make up our days. Very long I am beginning to find them, although we have some very pleasant people on board. After dinner, and until late in the evening, there is generally a grand promenade on deck; some of the English ladies make a point of dressing for dinner, so that the deck has quite a gay appearance. As the evening wanes, the deck becomes comparatively cleared, and the saloon is filled with *coteries* and card-parties. The Spaniards are very noisy over their cards; so unlike the phlegmatic British, who generally are quietly absorbed in their games of whist.

We have a Peruvian general on board who has been engaged, I am told, in all the *pronunciamentos* of late years; he has lost one arm, and altogether has much the appearance of a bandit. He was taken dangerously ill last night, and no wonder, for it is reported that he drank twenty-four glasses of brandy and soda in the course of the day. There is also a most amusing little fat man, a Spaniard of Porto Rico, as broad as he is long. Groups of admirers surround him whenever he appears, and roar at every expression that falls from him. He is certainly very quaint in his diction; his broken English gives a piquancy to his expressions, but he is not over choice in his words or sentiments. I believe the Spaniards are innate gamblers; they collect in a quiet part of the lower deck, and there till the lights are extinguished they play at *monte*. I have seen the table covered with silver. Gambling is not allowed on board; the Captain, in his quiet way, knows of everything that takes place, but I fancy he winks at this, as long as it is conducted quietly, and no complaints are made.

July 7*th.*—Our progress through the water has not been so rapid as it ought to have been. To-day at noon only 257 knots have been made in the four-and-twenty hours. A lottery is organized every morning on the result.

I am sorry to hear that there are three cases of small-pox among the stokers. It is important to keep these matters secret; but that is difficult, seeing how every one looks out for something to tell. We understand that the patients are doing well, and that they are kept entirely separate from the rest of the crew. But what matters that? the surgeon must visit them, and he associates much with us. Mothers feel anxious, and Mr. and Mrs. Dismal predict that we shall be in quarantine at Southampton. The Captain thinks not; but he is a cautious man, and speaks little about the affairs of the ship.

I had a long conversation with Mr. Latimer, the United States Consul at Porto Rico. He is a pleasant, intelligent person, and the only decorated Yankee I ever met. He always wears an order, a Spanish one I presume, at his button-hole.*

Poor Mr. Jerningham gets worse and worse. I notice a daily change in him; I fear that he will never be better.

(I am sorry to say he died on reaching the Hotel at Southampton.)

Wednesday, July 8th.—I jumped out of bed before five o'clock, being aroused by cries of "Murder, murder"! The waiters, who were already at work in cleaning the saloon, seemed bewildered. Upon inquiry it turned out to be a seaman who was "bad in his head." I was told afterwards that he was one of the small-pox patients,

* Since dead. He sank under a surgical operation at Paris.

and had escaped from the sick-bay; so I arose and took my bath. The mornings are getting more chilly now, and there is a consequent diminution in the numbers of the bathers.

We are getting on faster now. We made 284 knots yesterday, and the same to-day. These mail-boats always arrive to their time, although our ship is said to be foul at the bottom, and the screw not quite in order.

A "school" of porpoises, father, mother, and a numerous young family, were tumbling over and over within a stone's throw of us. I presume this term "school" is derived from the old Saxon word *Shole* (*Sceole*, A. S.), and not because Pa and Ma are enjoying the delightful task of teaching the young ideas how to gyrate. I think the word might be so spelt as to avoid confusion.

The weather has been damp and hazy all day, but the night proved beautiful. The sky was brilliant with stars, absolutely dazzling. There was Venus descending rapidly to the sea, shedding a flood of light across the water like the angels' path to heaven of which we have read. A deep bank of clouds resting on the horizon had all the appearance of mountains, silvery lakes, and towns; so that in imagination one might picture them to be the "Islands of the Blest."

But what chiefly attracts attention is a comet. I am not quite sure for how many nights it has been visible to us. But our pleasant acquaintance, Mr. B—— of Barbadoes, who brought the last file of the *Times* on board, points out to us a notice of it in the paper of the 6th of June. We learn that it was discovered by M. Coggia, at the observatory of Marseilles, on 17th of April, and its position is accurately described just where we see it.

At length we descend to the saloon, now nearly deserted, and Captain M—— gives us a practical exposition of brewing whisky toddy on scientific principles.

Thursday, July 9th.—I had to close the port last night for the first time, and required some extra clothing on the bed. How I shall regret the lovely enjoyable weather we have had! There is nothing particular to note to-day. Some Mother Carey's chickens crossed our wake. The Peruvian general seems all "a taunto" again, and is deeply engaged in *monte* below. The bows of the steamer are strewed with turtle, and some of them are put out of the way, in a sort of safe, with wire grating, amidst other live animals. There they lie neglected unless a poke or kick is administered to test their liveliness. No food, no water; I am told the mortality among them during 'a voyage home is generally fifty per cent. I always consider a turtle's lot is as hard as its shell. What a miserable existence! Our day's progress has been 280 knots.

At 7.30. P.M. we were passing the Azores—"Ilhos dos Açores," a name said to be derived from the number of hawks by which they were frequented on their discovery, which the natives called *açores*. They are the only islands that lie in the North Atlantic between Europe and America. The group consists of nine islands, widely scattered, extending over 300 miles; they are 795 miles from the west coast of Portugal, to which they belong, and contained in 1868 a population of over 250,000. On our starboard beam is the small island of St. Mary; and then we come to several barren rocks called the Formigas, or Ants, of volcanic appearance. St. Michael's, so famous for oranges, is now looming on the port-side, but we can see but little of it. One of the ship's officers tells me that there is a great depth of water all round with no harbour, and navigation is dangerous. Pico (so called from its peak), farther to the westward, rises to an apex of 7,000 feet. Sea-kings as we British consider ourselves, it is gratifying to our national vanity to know that amidst these islands, when in possession of the Spaniards, one of our early naval heroes, overwhelmed by numbers, yet most gloriously maintained the honour of his profession. It was in 1591 that a squadron of seven English ships, under Vice-Admiral Sir Richard Grenville, fell in with the Spanish squadron at the Azores. Grenville refused to make his escape by flight, and owing to his determined resistance the enemy took but one ship; the rest of the squadron returned safely to England. Sir Richard was surrounded by Spanish ships, and from the time the fight began, about three o'clock in the afternoon, to the break of day next morning, he repulsed the enemy fifteen times. In the beginning of the action he received a wound, but he continued doing his duty on deck till eleven at night, when receiving another he was carried below to have it dressed. During this operation a shot struck him in the head, and the surgeon was killed by his side. Powder began to fail, and the small arms had become broken or useless. The English at first were but 103, of whom 40 were killed, and almost all the rest wounded. The mast had gone by the board, and the ship was now an unmanageable hulk. In this situation Grenville proposed to destroy the ship and themselves rather than yield to the enemy, but, the proposal being opposed, he was obliged to surrender.

He died a few days after, and his last words were those of a hero: "Here die I, Richard Grenville, with a joyful and quiet mind, for that I have ended my life as a true soldier ought to do, fighting for his country, queen, religion, and honour. My soul willingly departing from this body, leaving behind the lasting fame of having behaved as every valiant soldier is in his duty bound to do."*

Tuesday, 14th.—The last three days have been very hazy; our progress, therefore, has been slow. The ship's bell has been kept ringing, and the steam whistle has repeatedly been sounded; the engines frequently stopped in order that the deep sea lead might be heaved and examined. We have been creeping onwards very cautiously. To-day the mist has disappeared, and the morning is bright and warm. The captain announces that the Lizard has been sighted. The passengers are all excited, letters are being written, telegrams prepared, and clothes packed.

We are running alongside the land, a barren-looking rocky coast—no waving palms, no verdant

* "Hackluyt's Voyages," vol. ii. p. 169.

savannas, no gorgeous hues of clustering plants; umbrageous solitudes there are, but these are chilly nooks where the sun never penetrates. I am not, however, in a discontented mood. "England, with all thy faults," I am delighted to see you again.

We have signalled to Lloyd's agent; so in a few minutes our arrival will be known in London and Southampton. We pass Falmouth, and the Eddystone; then we enter the Sound, pass the breakwater, and then we brought up in the grand harbour of Plymouth. I felt proud of the sight; the first impressions on the many foreign eyes on board must be favourable. Nor can I forget that at the bowling-green on the Hoe, Drake and Hawkins, Frobisher and Howard of Effingham—those great captains whose equals have never before been brought together—were assembled "when the dark cloud gathered round our coasts, in that agony of the Protestant faith and English name." I wonder if our Spanish passengers think of these things. Probably not.

There is great confusion on board. The tender comes alongside; an agent receives our numerous telegrams, and as he charges a shilling postage for each one, his trip will not be without profit. We hear nothing of quarantine or health-officers, although I suppose we have been visited. Upwards of one hundred passengers are leaving here, and great is the amount of luggage to be hauled out. At last the little tender steams off, we wave handkerchiefs and cheer. There they go, "jolly companions, every one," and probably we shall never meet again.

Then we get under weigh and steam out; follow the land to Start Point, and then shape our course across the Channel to Cherbourg. What an attenuated party we were at dinner. We talk over the departed, but there is something funereal about it; we linger over our wine, for there is nothing else to do. It is a lovely night, a bright moon and a calm sea, but the decks are bare; the gay throng of promenaders has vanished; in the saloon there reigns a dull quiet; the Englishmen are intent upon their newspapers, and there is no resource but to retire early to our berths.

Wednesday, 15*th.*—Awoke at 2 A.M. by the stopping of the engines. I look out of the port and see Cherbourg. Hasten on deck; pass the grand *digue,* which was considered a standing menace to England. The commerce of the place seems to have fallen off since I saw it in the days of the Empire, for there were but two vessels in the Port. We part with all our foreign passengers here.

It is difficult to recognise them now; the ladies are all dressed in their best attire, and men whom we have known only with loose jackets and wide-awakes are now set up in tight coats and tall hats, and all with walking-sticks, as if prepared for a promenade in the *Champs Elysées*. A smart little steamer, much better than the Plymouth one, takes them off; we give them a cheer which they return.

We are under weigh immediately. At breakfast-time the Needles are in sight; we pass, in rapid succession, all the well-known land-marks, looking bright and beautiful under the sunlight, and at 12 o'clock midday we are alongside the Southampton quay.

Farewells are exchanged and hands are pressed. Captain, officers, passengers, have all contributed something to the general comfort and amusement. I am sure they have to mine, and I am thankful at having returned in renewed health, after great enjoyment, with some information, and without accident, annoyance, or the least cause for disquietude.

THE END.

PRINTED BY VIRTUE AND CO., LIMITED, CITY ROAD, LONDON.

www.ingramcontent.com/pod-product-compliance
Lightning Source LLC
Chambersburg PA
CBHW030729230426

43667CB00007B/646